UNSUNG HEROES

UNSUNG HEROES

BY
Derek Elvin

International Headquarters
101 Queen Victoria Street, London EC4P 4EP

ISBN 978-0-85412-764-1

First published 2007

Cover artwork by Berni Georges
Line drawings by Lieut-Colonel Peter Dalziel
Produced by International Headquarters
Printed by UK Territory Print & Design Unit

CONTENTS

FOREWORD

THE Salvation Army has made a habit of discovering, recruiting and developing remarkable people. Rather, God has sent into its ranks the kind of people who were needed to do his work through this movement.

'*Heroes of the Faith*' (published in 2004) retold the stories of 12 pioneer leaders of the Army. Most came from its early years. This book is a sequel. It tells of some more recent 'Heroes'. They do not consider themselves heroic but as you read their stories you can catch a glimpse of the passion and commitment that marked their lives.

W. Stanley Cottrill

THE PRISONER

THE PRISONER
The story of W. Stanley Cottrill

'WE want you both to go to Manchuria,' said the Salvation Army leader to the two young captains. 'You will need to bring forward the date of your wedding and be ready to sail in June.'

The year was 1940. War was raging in Europe. Japan had invaded Manchuria and the people were being terrorised. All journeys by ship were highly dangerous because of the activity of submarines. No details of the voyage could be published for security reasons. There were no labels on their luggage. The route of their journey was kept secret. Not even their parents knew where they were going.

Stan Cottrill and Kathleen Ward had every reason to ask to be excused this assignment. They spoke no Mandarin or Cantonese. They had no knowledge of the culture of this Asian nation. They must have been aware of the dangers that faced them. But they went. They trusted their leaders, it is true, but their real trust was in God, to whom they had committed their lives. Obeying was a natural and simple outcome of that trust.

For 12 weeks the ship wandered its way around the world via Gibraltar, Cape Town (where they managed to find the Army headquarters), Mombasa, Bombay, Colombo, Singapore, Hong Kong and Shanghai, where they had to change ship for Mukden in Manchuria. Stan described it as a honeymoon but the daily threat of torpedoes, the heat and discomfort of a cargo vessel beng used as a troop ship and the unknown route must have concerned the young couple and caused them to be anxious.

It is not surprising that Stan Cottrill had an international outlook. His parents were Salvation Army officers from Britain. They were serving in South Africa when Stan was born and later transferred to New Zealand where Stan spent his teenage years. He learned a lot from their willingness to serve wherever they were wanted and from their example of compassionate caring. Indeed the whole family - parents, aunts, uncles and cousins - were involved in the 'permanent mission to the unconverted' that was The Salvation Army. In one sense it was almost inevitable that Stan would offer for officership and be willing to 'trust and obey', just as so many of his family and friends had done.

But the real reason for his sense of commitment came from his relationship with Jesus. As a small boy he sang 'my sins rose as high as a mountain'. This could hardly be true but he found the sense of forgiveness and peace that came from meeting Jesus for himself. In teenage years the profound holiness teaching of a Maori corps officer made an impact on his life as he knelt at the mercy seat seeking the blessing of a clean heart.

So naturally and simply, out of a love for the Lord who had given all for him, Stan responded to a sense of calling and entered the International Training college as a cadet in the 'Enthusiasts' session. It was here, in his second year, as the Assistant Cadet Sergeant-Major of the 'Dauntless Evangelists', that he made a decision that would shape his future life.

He had heard Olive Chester speak of her work in China, and the leader of the meeting had invited them to sing 'I'll go with him, all the way'. Stan responded at the mercy seat and noted the date and the chorus in his songbook. These simple words became the pattern for his life. Next day he wrote a letter volunteering for missionary service.

Manchuria was as difficult as Stan and Kathleen had expected. The Army was small and struggling. It had been hoped that they would be the training principals for this small command. But there was little time for the complex language studies that would have made their work practical. There was a serious danger that the Japanese authorities would react badly to the presence of

Europeans in the area. The political upheaval in the country made it impossible for them to establish their ministry. Before long the advice of local experts was taken and Stan and his bride were transferred to what was considered to be the safer appointment of Singapore.

Not that questions of safety were much in the thoughts of Stan and Kathleen! They wanted to get on with the service to which they felt called. God would look after them. So once again they trusted and obeyed and sailed back through dangerous waters via Hong Kong to Singapore.

They were appointed in charge of the boys' home. They quickly learned to love the abandoned and orphaned children who looked to them and their staff for the affection and care they so badly needed. Soon they had a child of their own and looked forward to a settled period of ministry as a family in this secure island fortress. After all, Singapore would not fall to the rapidly advancing Japanese forces. Churchill had said ' the island will not, must not fall'.

By the beginning of February 1942 it was clear that the future of Singapore was in the balance. Air raids and the sound of approaching troops were causing concern to everyone. The Governor ordered all European women and children to leave and Kathleen, with her eight-month-old son, and this time without Stan, boarded a ship for Australia. They left with one small suitcase and a pram. Stan was left on the quayside wondering when and if he would see his family again. It was to be a separation of three-and-a-half years. He might have had the opportunity of going with his wife and child but, along with the other men and four single women officers, he elected to stay with his people. Whatever their personal danger and suffering these Salvationists would continue to serve the community in the name of Christ.

On Sunday 15 February Lieut-General Percival surrendered to the Japanese forces. Within days Stan - together with his leaders

5

Herbert Lord and Charles Davidson, the other European officers and 2,000 civilians - was summoned to the cricket ground. 'You are the scum of the earth and deserve to die,' said the Japanese military commander, standing on a barrel in front of the crowd. 'But the emperor has decreed that you shall live.' Surrounded by soldiers with their loaded rifles, Stan admits to being afraid at this point but, in the week's notice given to him, he prepared basic goods for his imprisonment and took them in a vehicle to the muster point. He was able to assist some of the older people on the 14-mile march to Changi Prison where they were to be interned.

Changi Prison was built to accommodate 500 people and now it was filled to overflowing with 2,000 frightened internees. It could have led to chaos but committees were soon established, work responsibilities allocated and some order established by the internees themselves. The Japanese guards were very strict, demanding respect from their charges. Those who failed to give it were punished severely. It was a place of atrocity, loneliness, starvation and confinement. The food lacked protein and vegetables and was generally insufficient for the needs of the men. Many of those interned had lived comfortably affluent lives and they suffered badly under this regime.

Gradually the health of the internees grew worse and the demand for hospital services increased. Stan volunteered to work as a hospital orderly. Although he had no training he was required to serve in the operating theatre. His initial feeling of horror at what he witnessed was soon replaced by a competence which drew praise from the doctor for whom he worked. To have such an assistant was better than working with a colleague medical man, he said. Stan felt that this service was both profitable and satisfying.

Real opportunities to comfort and support the sick and dying came Stan's way. He was also able to take his turn in arranging and leading the services held in the camp. On one occasion the Bishop of Singapore, Leonard Wilson, and Stan were to lead a service. The bishop read the beautiful words of Christ's High Priestly prayer in John's Gospel. It made such an impression on the young Army officer that he determined that he would always give great attention to the reading of God's word in every meeting for which he was responsible.

Stan had learned that Kathleen and their child had arrived safely in Australia just before he was interned but he was unable to get news to her of his own situation. It was two years before he was allowed to send a 25-word postcard giving the news that he had survived.

In such a lonely situation it was vital that all Christians should guard their spiritual health. There was a shortage of books in the camp but those who had some agreed to share them in a small library. Stan found a copy of J M Baillie's *Diary of Private Prayer*. It was such an inspiration that he decided to write it out by hand so that he could retain a copy for his own use. Its formal prayers often provided for Stan's needs when his own words were hard to find. A regular time of shared prayer with his officer colleagues at the end of every day, and a Bible study group which met under the stars, were further means by which Stan retained and enhanced his relationship with Jesus. A fellow internee from a Brethren background agreed to memorise a passage of Scripture every week for the group to discuss.

In moments of anxiety and stress Stan found encouragement from Bishop Wilson whose maturity and wisdom helped the young captain to regain his spiritual poise.

It is hard to imagine that anything positive could come out of an experience like this but, speaking of it many years later, Stan was able to quote the words of Joseph to his brothers in Genesis 50:20: 'You meant it for evil but God meant it for good.' He emerged from Changi stronger in his faith, having discovered fellowship with great Christians of other traditions, and with little or no hatred or bitterness towards those who had interned him. Surely his trust in the Lord had been justified.

When Singapore was liberated Stan remained for a while in the internment camp. It was not yet safe to return to the stricken city but, as soon as possible, the officers who had been interned returned to their responsibilities. After all, they had elected to stay in Singapore for the sake of the people and so their first thoughts were for those who had suffered under Japanese rule. Along with his colleagues, Stan agreed to remain in Singapore for a further six months. They shared accommodation and worked together. During this period the Army in Singapore was reborn, with former soldiers returning and new people won for the Lord. Many had experienced dreadful hardship and suffering but Stan and his colleagues searched for them, found them and encouraged them to return. Those six months were a heavy price to pay for Stan and Kathleen who had already been separated for three-and-a-half years, but Stan felt that they were worth it.

Finally, a military flight to Brisbane saw Stan and Kathleen and their son Derek reunited again. They were able to stay with Stan's parents, now appointed to Australia. Six months' furlough gave them the opportunity to renew and rebuild their lives and to share their story with fellow Salvationists in many Australian corps.

Where next for the Cottrills? Would they be given a quiet, gentle appointment in their homeland to recuperate? Typically they accepted an appointment to return to Singapore and help the people to rebuild their shattered community. Once more it was a question of 'trust and obey'. For five more years they served there. Stan became a probation officer, working with young people who had broken the law, offering support and guidance. Some of these young men found fellowship at the Army corps and some became Salvation Army soldiers.

Then Stan and Kathleen became the corps officers for Singapore Central Corps. There they ministered to the local people and welcomed into their home many young men from Britain undertaking their national service. This was a very busy appointment with all the joys and frustrations of a corps officer's work. In all Stan gave 12 years of his life to the people of Singapore in the most difficult period of their history.

Where would 'trust and obey' lead them next? Following a brief holiday in England, Stan and Kathleen were appointed to what was then Rhodesia. They spent the next 10 years working there. Stan was appointed as the divisional commander in two rural divisions. Among his varied responsibilities, this involved him in visiting the many corps and schools under his direction. He would set off on a Monday morning for a distant corps in the 'bush' where inspections and meetings were to be held. Overnight he would sleep in the truck or a hut made available to him, and then move on next day to the next centre, returning home at the end of the week. He quickly came to identify with the people. Many were coping with problems of poverty and ignorance. He understood and sought to help. In turn they came to respect and love him.

The educational programme provided by the Army was the means of helping very many African young people to gain skills urgently needed by their community. Many became significant leaders of their people. It was made possible by a programme of teacher training offered at the Howard Institute in rural Rhodesia. This provided the highly skilled and motivated teachers for all the Army schools. For four years Stan was the principal of this institute, directing and inspiring those who would be the teachers of their people. Alongside the many excellent overseas officers who provided the professional training, Stan's spiritual leadership and wisdom enhanced the reputation of 'Howard' in the nation. On Sunday morning he would have the privilege of regularly leading worship for the 500 students from the central primary school and the teacher training college. What an impact this made on many young lives! As he watched these student teachers march by he thought of the impact they would make on the youth of their nation and prayed for them.

Many officers who have served in Africa say that it 'gets under your skin'. Stan's affection for the African Salvationists and his love for the land that has seen so much suffering and conflict is still evident. He was able to adapt to a very different culture and to understand the needs of the people. Part of his heart remained with the people of that land.

Ten years' service in rural Africa was followed by a brief appointment at the Army's International Headquarters. Then, in 1964 there came what may be seen as the greatest challenge to the principle of 'trust and obey' that Stan and Kathleen adopted. The Army asked them to go to Japan. Stan was to be second in command to the godly Commissioner Hasegawa. At their farewell meeting from IHQ a colleague officer said, 'Here is a man who was a *prisoner* of the Japanese, who is now being sent to be a *servant* of the Japanese.' The gracious, loving spirit with which Stan and Kathleen went enabled them to win the hearts of the people. In this land where Christians are in such a small minority, they soon found themselves in the middle of a warm, caring group of fellow Salvationists with whom they had much in common.

There was much to learn. It was yet another change of culture. This time the traditions were different from any they had previously met. The language barrier meant that they had to rely on translators for all their public speaking and interviews. Commissioner Hasegawa was a sick man and this meant that an increasing burden of responsibility fell on Stan's shoulders. The children had to face another change of school programmes. Yet Stan counts this as one of the most satisfying and fulfilling periods of his ministry. As the Japanese nation developed into a successful manufacturing society, so Stan and the loyal and faithful Japanese Salvationists reminded the nation of the God of love who sent Jesus as the Saviour of the world. A reflection of that love was surely to be seen in the forgiving and accepting spirit of the English couple who served among them.

Stan's international understanding and wise leadership were being increasingly recognised by the Army's leadership. So it was not surprising that, after five valuable years in Japan, the Cottrill family were called back to London. Stan was to serve in a key position as Chief Secretary to the Army's Second in Command. It was not without some sadness that they left the Land of the Rising Sun. In his new task Stan would see the needs of the whole world, with all its diversity and problems, come across his desk. The world was changing fast. The Army had constantly to adapt. New solutions to the challenges had to be found. From his desk at Queen Victoria Street, Stan used his wide experience to help the forward movement of Christ's Kingdom through the Army.

One more opportunity to serve overseas remained. Kathleen and Stan were appointed as the territorial leaders to Korea. In many ways this was the hardest time for them. This act of 'trust and obedience' would take them to yet another cultural change, another difficult language, at a critical time in the history of a nation. And this time they would have to leave their family behind in England.

In nearly 20 years since the ending of the Korean War, the South Korean republic had seen massive changes. The beginnings of economic prosperity had changed the lives of many people and the growth of the Christian Church had profoundly altered the situation for the Army. The influence of missionaries who had made a long-term commitment to the Army in Korea had ensured that the territory had a number of very fine potential leaders. Stan's task, as the last 'missionary' leader for the territory, was to pave the way for the first Korean national leader. It required great skill, teaching and mentoring ability and a gracious spirit as he 'worked himself out of a job'.

Once again Stan and Kathleen showed the spirit of caring leadership which was appreciated by the Korean Salvationists.

The remaining years of Stan and Kathleen' service were to be centred on International Headquarters but this was no time to settle down into a desk-based routine. As International Secretary for Africa and the Far East, Stan now had a parish which included all the countries in which he had served and many more. He and

Kathleen visited most, if not all, of them, encouraging, challenging, leading congresses, commissioning officers, planning future developments. Such a schedule would have daunted a younger couple but the Cottrills rose to its challenges with quiet grace and unquenchable enthusiasm.

When Commissioner Arnold Brown was elected as the Army's 11th General it was not surprising that he asked Stan to be his Chief of the Staff. He needed a man of the widest experience of a world of need, someone who would keep calm and balanced in the midst of any crisis that might occur. He needed a man whose gracious and gentle manner would commend itself to all but whose determination to do the right would not be deflected. Above all he needed someone who had demonstrated how to trust God in the most difficult situations and still find the grace to obey. Stan and Kathleen once again saluted and obeyed, carrying the heavy burdens of this massive responsibility with integrity and patience.

One final act of trust and obedience saw Stan agree to serve an extra six months after his retirement date in order to help the new General enter office.

Then began the fruitful years of retirement as he became the elder statesman at the corps where he soldiered. He always offered encouragement and support to the officers, local officers and especially to the young people. He became involved with the Bible Society and the many activities of the corps which kept him busy.

The sudden, unexpected promotion to Glory of Kathleen in 1988 was a blow, for this loving partnership in marriage had been a strength to them both. Surviving the stresses of separation and constant change, they had come to rely on each other as they sought to serve their Lord. But Stan accepted his loss, learned to lean even more on his Saviour and found the grace to carry on alone.

When Stan was asked to lead a meeting in prayer, whether at the full-to-capacity holiness meeting or the small Bible study group, those who shared in the prayer sensed that he was talking simply and honestly to a friend. He had known his Saviour for so long and at such depth that the intimacy and love that flowed through the words became an inspiration for all who listened. In a life of trust, God's unfailing grace had been proved.

The promise, made at the very beginning of Stan's officership, remained as a guiding star throughout his long life. 'I'll go with him, all the way' meant a dangerous voyage to Manchuria, a prison camp in Singapore, 10 years of hard work in rural Africa, service to the nation of his former captors and the demands of a rapidly changing Korean nation. It led to a sharing of the heavy responsibilities of worldwide leadership. It meant a life of simple trust and willingness to obey. It brought great fulfilment and friendship with people from every part of the world. He had no regrets about the commitment he made, only gratitude to God for all his leadings.

'…There's no other way to be happy in Jesus, but to trust and obey.'

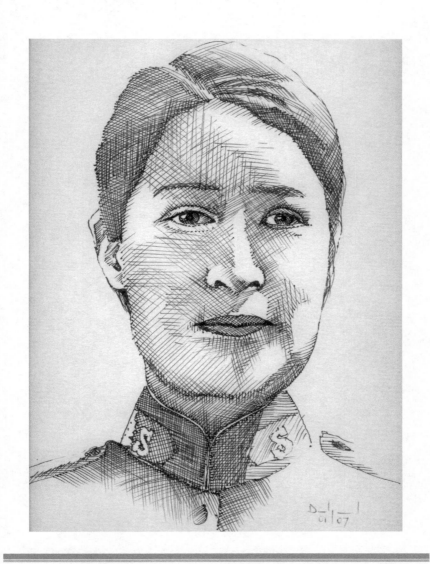

Rin Iwasa

THE REBELLIOUS DAUGHTER

THE REBELLIOUS DAUGHTER
The story of Rin Iwasa

IT all started when Rin Iwasa was 15 years old. She was presiding at the family's serene Japanese tea ceremony. It was not the time or the place to cause a shock. But she had some important news to share and it could not wait.

Rin was the daughter of respected, aristocratic parents. Although her father observed all the traditions of the Buddhist-Shintoist faith, he was an enlightened man and had offered her the best education that could be found. She was tall, slim and attractive, a brilliant student who had graduated from high school at the age of 15 in the year 1906. The family were very proud of her.

Now she simply had to break the news. 'Father, I want to be a doctor,' she said. Such a career for a well brought up Japanese girl in the 19th century was unheard of. She feared that her mother's dreams of a beautiful wedding, a handsome son-in-law and a large family over which she might preside would be shattered.

To Rin's amazement her father smiled his agreement. 'I am not surprised. I thought you would make this choice long ago. You will be a doctor to my Buddhist friends here in Nagoya,' he said. 'Then you will marry another doctor in the town and our family will be complete.' Even Rin's mother seemed pleased with the idea.

Rin was one of the earliest girl students at the Tokyo Medical School. Already she was breaking with family traditions and expectations. As a child she had read stories about Florence Nightingale and pictured herself bringing healing like the famous nurse.

A new lecturer was to join the staff of the medical school and Rin, along with other students was invited to meet him. He was Dr Sanya Matsuda, the only Christian among the teachers at the school. Meeting his students for the first time he told them, 'In medical men and women of any nation, character is important. The best preparation for a medical career is the knowledge of Jesus Christ.'

He spoke about Dr David Livingstone giving up his medical practice in Britain to pioneer work in Africa. 'There are 70 million people in Japan. Right here in Tokyo, thousands of the very poor suffer the miseries of tuberculosis because they can't afford treatment. Look no further for a mission field.'

Dr Matsuda was not popular with his fellow professors. They did not like his direct approach to religion and were concerned about his influence on the students. But Rin Iwasa was convinced by his modesty, sincerity and commitment. She led a group of students who would make their way to Dr Matsuda's simple rooms to hear more of his understanding of medicine and life.

It soon emerged that Dr Matsuda was a Salvationist. 'They call him "Christ-like Matsuda",' said one of Rin's fellow students. He had given up a very profitable practice to become the superintendent of a hospital for the poorest people in the city. Rin began to study books about Christianity and the strange new movement to Japan called The Salvation Army. This was all very new to the young woman who had been brought up carefully in the strict Buddhist-Shintoist philosophy of her parents.

Eventually the day of Rin's graduation came. Now she was Dr Rin Iwasa. Her family were naturally delighted to see how well she had done. Surely she would return to her home city and begin her work among the wealthy clients her father had already marked out for her care.

Once more Rin had to face the ordeal of breaking news to her father. 'I want to join the team working with Dr Matsuda at the Salvation Army hospital. We will care for the very poorest of people in the slums of our capital city.' This time her father did not smile his approval. Rin had to fight a bitter battle with the family. She described the two months struggle as 'days of agony'.

Eventually she won her father's consent to return to Tokyo and to begin her work. But on no account was she to become a Salvationist. Her father thought that, before long, she would tire of this demanding work and would want to return home.

The work was hard. Dr Matsuda had begun a programme to visit the poorest people in their homes. Rin discovered poverty and deprivation on a scale which she had not believed possible. Once she found a shed with 60 people living inside, all were suffering from tuberculosis. Such conditions were offensive to a young woman brought up in comparative luxury but Rin faced the stench and misery with determination and loving care.

Later there was a measles outbreak in Tokyo and Rin was called on to provide heroic service. Two desperate mothers arrived with babies strapped to their backs. One had died on the way to the hospital and the other was critically ill.

Rin determined to go to see for herself the living conditions. She found a windowless hovel with 18 people living there. She had to use a torch to examine them for no light penetrated the room. No one there had money to pay for a doctor. She found that one of the mothers had already lost four children to the disease. Rin rolled up her sleeves and with the help of her nurses offered the best treatment she could to the suffering people.

In these first years Rin worked incessantly at the hospital. The records show that she never took a day off work or had holidays. She continually thanked God for giving her the strength to do her work. The overwhelming needs of the people and the love she felt for them sustained her.

Rin Iwasa had found her life's work among the poor of the city. But this conviction still did not receive the blessing of her family. Rin's announcement that she wished to become a Christian was greeted with dismay by her parents. Her mother was distraught as

19

she prayed at the family shrine. She still hoped that Rin would return to her home town and settle down to a traditional life there.

Instead, without asking her father's permission, Rin journeyed to London to attend The Salvation Army's International Congress in 1914. The long boat journey provided her with time to reflect. One night, as she walked the deck of the ship she felt the presence of Jesus and accepted him as Saviour and Lord. This would be the defining moment of her life. She would obey her Lord even if it meant conflict and separation from her family.

Rin stayed on in London after the congress to train as a Salvation Army officer. Upon her commissioning she was appointed back to her homeland and returned to her work at the hospital under the direction of Dr Matsuda.

As Rin and others of the hospital team visited the people in their homes they became aware of the frequency with which they found tuberculosis among the poor people. A later article in the Japanese *War Cry* showed that the problem was much more severe than in other parts of the world. The team became convinced of the need for a specialist hospital and sanatorium to help those who were suffering from the disease. The purpose-built sanatorium at Suginami was opened in 1916 and Rin was appointed to this new work. It was the first such hospital dedicated to those who could not pay for treatment.

The new hospital pioneered a totally different approach to the needs of the patients. Some were so sick that they needed hospital care but, as they began to recover, another kind of help was needed. Small huts were built in the wooded grounds of the sanatorium and there the patients were helped to recover at their own pace.

Instead of being sent back to the competitive world of industry they were allowed to develop and use their skills in a sheltered place. Soon the hospital grounds were being used to raise pigs and chickens, to grow flowers and crops, to mend shoes or cut hair, and to repair electrical goods. The patients received good food and lived in a quiet environment. Their health steadily improved until they were well enough to go home.

The new idea came from the great mind of Dr Matsuda and it was Rin Iwasa who helped it blossom. Alongside the occupational therapy Rin and Dr Matsuda had the opportunity of talking to their patients about Jesus Christ and leading them into faith. This view of healthy and holy living was the greatest gift that could be given to those coping with the deadly disease.

By this time the world was in the grip of the First World War but the international struggle was made worse for Rin by renewed hostility from her family. She was bombarded with letters, calls and telegrams demanding that she return home. For five years she endured the pleas and anger of those she loved. They would have admired such dedication in other people but could not accept it in their own daughter. They feared for her health and deplored the conditions in which she worked.

The stress this must have caused Rin was immense but those who worked with her saw only a calm peace, an encouraging smile and a selfless willingness to care for others. She never wavered in her devotion to God and the work to which he had called her. The sanatorium became a model for such work throughout Japan and Rin's care for the spiritual as well as the physical needs of her patients was admired by all who came into contact with her.

Dr Iwasa worked closely with Dr Matsuda as the sanatorium expanded. She became the assistant superintendent as the hospital grew from 50 to 260 patients. Every year saw the number of patients increase and the expertise of the staff developed to meet a variety of needs.

In 1923 Rin Iwasa was honoured by The Salvation Army with the Order of the Founder. The citation for the award read: 'For compassionate and devoted toil amongst sufferers from tuberculosis in Japan, and in the establishment of a sanatorium in Tokyo.'

Seven years later her mentor, Sanya Matsuda, was promoted to Glory. Who would be asked to succeed him in the leadership of medical work in Japan? No woman officer had been given such a heavy responsibility but it was to Rin Iwasa that the Army leaders naturally turned. No one else had the knowledge, and the commitment to see this wonderful work develop. She was appointed as superintendent of Suginami Sanatorium in Tokyo.

Rin had been greatly influenced by Sanya Matsuda. She wrote of him: 'He was a really humble person and never wanted his name to be recognised by the public. He did not see it important to be complimented on his work.' These qualities of self-effacing humility and conscientious hard work were shown equally in the life of Rin Iwasa as in the man who had taught her.

She not only managed the work in the original hospital and the sanatorium but also soon became aware that even these facilities were inadequate for the needs of the Tokyo poor. So the next stage was to find a site for another, larger sanatorium. Tirelessly Rin visited 30 possible sites to negotiate with their owners and to deal with neighbours who were reluctant to have such a hospital in their area. Finally a site was found and the new sanatorium was built in the Kiyose suburb of Tokyo.

In addition to her already heavy workload, Rin took responsibility for this new development. By the time it was ready to open its doors to the many sick people who needed its resources the world was again at war.

Rin had to face the immense problems of establishing this new hospital while The Salvation Army was being proscribed in her homeland as a 'foreign organisation'. The spiritual work of the Army became part of 'The Church of Christ in Japan' and the Army's social work had to be formed into another organisation called 'Love Neighbour Organisation'.

The Japanese Government took over the two hospitals and allowed Rin to continue managing and supervising their work.

By now she was caring for more than 400 patients at a time and overseeing 100 members of staff.

During these difficult years Rin kept her hope and faith alive. She worshipped with the Salvationists, always conscious of the presence of secret police at the meetings. No comments were allowed that might have offended against the emperor worship. She could not wear her uniform but she encouraged the thousands of Japanese Salvationists who hid their flags and uniforms, waiting for the day when they could be used again. With other colleagues she was a beacon of hope for those who might easily have despaired.

At the end of the war she was one of the 200 officers who petitioned the General to re-open The Salvation Army's work in Japan. Months later she was able to greet international leaders as they revisited her homeland.

The coming of peace meant a massive task of rebuilding. Rin was soon involved. By now she was an honoured figure in her nation. She had been awarded the Emperor's Medal with Blue Ribbon on behalf of The Salvation Army's work and had been invited to lecture at the Imperial Palace on her work combating tuberculosis.

In April 1948 she was in the thick of a great relief operation, giving treatment to victims of a great flood which devastated huge areas of the Kanto plain on the outskirts of Tokyo.

More than all the honours that came to her both nationally and from The Salvation Army, Rin was most pleased that her parents, who had once opposed her work, now recognised her achievements and were so proud of what their daughter had accomplished.

Thirty-five long years of selfless service took their toll on Rin's health. She had frequently put her own life at risk as she cared for those suffering from contagious diseases. Rin was forced to retire a little early from her position as the superintendant of the Army's two TB sanatoriums.

In 1949 Rin Iwasa became ill and was promoted to Glory on 19 June. She had been among those who had opened doors of service for women in Japan. She had kept her faith despite opposition from her family and her nation. She had challenged the conventions of her restrictive upbringing to become a heroine of her nation and of the faith she found in Jesus Christ.

Her work, and that of Dr Matsuda, was instrumental in dealing with the chronic problems of tuberculosis among Japan's poor. Innovations in treatment and care paved the way for the eradication of the disease as a major health hazard.

Today the influence of The Salvation Army is Japan is far greater than the relatively small number of its members might suggest. When new groundbreaking projects are required the Government often asks the Army to be responsible. When other agencies run into difficulty it is to the Army that they turn. Recent developments have seen the opening of the first hospice for terminally ill cancer patients in Tokyo.

Why is this movement, a tiny fraction of the very small Japanese Christian community, trusted in this way? The answer, at least in part, lies in the dedication to Jesus Christ and the commitment to the people shown by those who served in its hospitals and to Rin Iwasa in particular. Her parents had every right to be proud of the daughter who dared to challenge them and lived selflessly for others.

Lalkiamlova

THE LIBERATOR

THE LIBERATOR
The story of Lalkiamlova and Lalhlimpuii

THE 18-year-old freedom fighter wept as he knelt at the mercy seat in the prayer hall of his village. For three years he had been a member of the political group demanding independence for Mizoram. The last year had seen them hiding in the jungle, carrying their weapons and preparing to take on the might of the Indian Army.

Lalkiamlova's mother had been distraught about her son's involvement in the violent struggle. She had pleaded with his commander to stop him from being involved in the fighting and her determination had ensured that he had been kept out of the front line. But the price of belonging to such a group was absolute loyalty. He was bound to keep the secrets of the group. They would surely never let him leave. He knew too much. Even to ask could lead to his execution.

Lalkiamlova had been brought up in a Christian home. His grandparents had been Salvation Army officers. In his hilltop village with his family, he lived a simple life from his birth in 1949. He had knelt at the mercy seat in a children's meeting at the age of 10. There and then he met his saviour, Jesus, made his simple confession, learned the promises and become a junior soldier and later a corps cadet.

Then came the insurrection and Lalkiamlova's involvement in the complicated political struggles of his nation. The Mizos were unlike any of the other Indian people. Their land was in the far north-east of the country, separated from the rest of India by East Pakistan (now Bangladesh). Centuries before they had come from Mongolia and settled in the rugged, fertile hill-country then known as the Lushai Hills.

Christian missions had come to their land and many of the old animist practices had been replaced with a fervent faith. The Salvation Army pioneered work in the remote villages and now had thousands of active Salvationists. Perhaps it was understandable that these different people should want their own nation but the fight was hopeless and it seemed that young Lalkiamlova was trapped in an impossible struggle.

One day he attended a Salvation Army house-to-house campaign in his village. As he sat in the meeting in a neighbour's home, he heard the voice of God say to him, 'I want you to work for my Kingdom, not an earthly kingdom. You do not have to liberate the people, you simply have to point them to Jesus. True freedom is to be found in him.'

Late that night he made his way to the prayer hall at the highest point of the village. There, in the pitch-black darkness, he knelt at the same mercy seat he had used as a young boy. He promised he would serve the Lord for the rest of his life. But could he be released from his commitment to the freedom fighters?

Dare he speak to his commander? The risks were great and it took a long time for Lalkiamlova to gain the courage to make his request. As he thought about it, he was captured by the Indian military authorities. Despite their detailed questioning they could not prove he was a member of the insurgent group. Then he was caught for a second time, severely beaten and released. Now he knew he must speak to his commander.

'I have been called by God to serve him and to bring the message of his love to the people,' said the young man. Much to his surprise the commander replied, 'If God has called you, then I must release you.' What is more, the commander gave him a written note freeing him from further obligations to the group.

Returning to his home the way seemed clear. He read an article in *The War Cry* from a divisional leader in a different Indian state, far from his homeland and people: 'Whether you are educated or not, we need volunteers who will take the gospel to the poorest people. An opportunity exists for people to serve as teachers and evangelists in an area where there is great darkness and sin. Who will respond?' Immediately Lalkiamlova and his best friend agreed that they would go. Leaving their home village they made the long journey to meet the divisional leader and offer their services.

When they arrived for their interview they were bitterly disappointed. 'You are too young. You do not speak the language. You have no money. You will never survive. I cannot give you any money for a salary and I have no place for you to live. This area is full of malaria. Who will give you medicine? Go home and forget about it.' Without even a prayer the divisional leader dismissed them, but then said: 'You can stay overnight. Pray and study your Bible. If you still want to do this work, I will meet you in front of my house at six in the morning.'

The two friends were devastated. They hardly knew how to pray. All their enthusiasm and energy drained away. They were angry at the unsympathetic response of the man whose article had encouraged them. Their total resources would support them for less than a month. How should they react to the leader's words? Perhaps he was right and they should go home.

Early next morning Lalkiamlova woke and asked his friend 'What shall we do?' 'I'm not coming,' replied the other man but Lalkiamlova said, 'I still feel that God wants me to do this work. I will report as he told us.'

Arriving at the house, Lalkiamlova found the divisional leader waiting for him with his bags packed and ready to go. He shouted a great 'Hallelujah'. Lalkiamlova realised that the previous day had been a test and that he had won a battle with himself. He said, 'I am determined to obey God's call for me.'

They set off by bus to travel to the area picked out for the new development. When they reached the nearest corps, the officer there and the divisional leader decided on the village which was to be the new outreach. It was a desperately poor place where there was no Christian presence. Here Lalkiamlova was to commence his ministry.

He discovered that to speak to the people he would have to learn two dialects of a new language. He found that there was no house in which he could live so, at first, he stayed with one of the families. Since he had no money this was a drain on the family's meagre resources so after a time it was agreed that all the members of the village would make a small contribution to his upkeep. Later Lalkiamlova built a small house for himself.

In order to pay his way he worked at cutting the sungrass which was used to roof the houses and sold it to buy food. A friendly Christian family from a nearby village gave him fruit and seeds and he lived on this simple fare for a long time.

In the first year of Laliamlova's work the divisional leader could only give him 20 rupees (about £1) for his work. With this he built a school and became its first teacher. The children became interested in the gospel. One young man helped him with the very hard work of cutting and carrying the sungrass to make the roof for a small prayer hall in which his people could worship the Lord Jesus.

One of the most demanding tasks for this young evangelist was to help his people understand what it meant to be a Christian. Often he would be asked how they should behave. What is the Christian way of grieving after a death? How should a body be buried? How do Christians celebrate a new birth? The young evangelist had to become all things to his people.

After a year a crisis occurred for the young evangelist. He was invited to present a gospel message to a family which had not yet become Christians. After his devotions the family distributed refreshment including some alcoholic drinks which, he later found, had been sacrificed to the devil because of a family sickness. When the drink was offered to him he refused; but some of his own Christian people, who were drunk themselves, pressed him to take the brew. He walked out of the meeting distressed beyond measure.

Making his way out of the village and into the bamboo jungle he said to God, 'Tell me tonight if you wish me to continue my ministry here. If you want me to leave the place, I will go tomorrow morning. All the work that I have done has been destroyed tonight. Tell me what I should do. How can I go on with these people? Shall I give up and return home? I need a word from you to tell me what to do'.

Lalkiamlova returned secretly to the village to find the people very distressed. They thought he had abandoned them and were desperate to find him. The young people had set out with bamboo torches to find him in the next village. One older man had not been present at the party. When Lalkiamlova found him he was told how much the people needed his ministry. 'Don't go away, we need you,' he said, his eyes filled with tears. Later Lalkiamlova recognised this word as the authentic word from God and stayed with his people.

Shortly after this episode Lalkiamlova received a message to say that his mother and sister were at the divisional headquarters asking for him. He hurried to meet them and learned that the military authorities had burned the whole village and that the family had lost all their possessions and been deported to a village far from their home.

Lalkiamlova took his mother and sister back with him to stay in the little house he had built. In these crowded conditions they stayed for a month. Then his mother suggested they should all return to Mizoram, their home state. What a dilemma for Lalkiamlova! If he fulfilled his family responsibility he would abandon the people who had become Christians through his ministry. They were not yet strong enough and would return to their old faith. What should he do?

Lalkiamlova's mother was not serious in her request. She was glad when her son confirmed his calling. He accompanied his

31

mother and sister to the borders of Mizoram and left them there to make their own way back home. The Lord honoured Lalkiamlova's commitment and kept all the family safe. It was another very hard test for the young man.

Lalkiamlova stayed at this first, voluntary appointment for three years. The people came to support him to the best of their ability. The school and the church began to grow. Then, in 1970, an opportunity came for the young man to enter The Salvation Army's training college. He almost refused the opportunity because he did not feel a specific call to officership. His call was to be an evangelist, a preacher.

Nevertheless he went to the college and found the way to serve God even more effectively through his officership. He was not the first choice for a place in the Lightbringers Session but one cadet did not arrive for training and Lalkiamlova was offered his place after the session had started.

Training involved practical work as well as studies. Lalkiamlova and other cadets conducted a campaign at one of the nearby corps. He had been told of the fine group of young people there and, in particular, about a young woman. Even before he met her Lalkiamlova was impressed by what he was told. She was a Sunday school teacher and wanted to become an officer.

This was the beginning of a deepening relationship with Lalhlimpuii that would lead to their marriage and to a wonderful partnership in sharing the gospel. Lalhlimpuii was trained in the Blood and Fire Session of cadets.

Following commissioning in 1971 Lieutenant Lalkiamlova was appointed to a village not too far from his earlier work. Now he had to learn yet another language for his work and discovered that he must once again be the teacher at the Army's school. Eighteen months later Lalhlimpuii (Puii) joined him and they began their ministry together.

This first corps was in a small village where all the people were very poor. Often the young officers gave away their own food to help families where the children were starving. Once Lalkiamlova made a journey to a relative to ask for some rice. When he returned after four days it was to find that Puii had parted with their last reserves of food for a starving family.

The area in which the corps was situated was prone to many diseases. Lalkiamlova and Puii both contracted malaria and were seriously ill. Puii's parents were afraid she would die and begged her to return home. There was little medical care available. The nearest medical centre was about 40 miles away. In order to get Puii some treatment her husband and the village men had to carry her to the flooded river and then get her across on a bamboo raft to find a doctor. Despite these problems they both rejoiced in the unshakeable faith of their people.

A second corps appointment followed. This is where their first child was born. Without the help of a trained doctor or midwife the young wife had a healthy baby girl in the simple house in which they lived. During this appointment Lalkiamlova served the divisional outreach evangelism board as secretary and used his earlier experience and enthusiasm to promote new developments in the area.

Then Lalkiamlova was asked to train as a teacher for the blind. The Government of Mizoram had asked The Salvation Army to establish and run the first programme to educate blind children in the state. Lalkiamlova quickly mastered the Braille system, adapting its use to the unique characters of his language.

He says that it was blind children who taught him how to walk with them and guide them and that he learned most from their experience. He transcribed all the primary school textbooks into Braille in the Mizo language. His expertise in this area is still recognised and he is often asked to develop the system further for use in his own language.

As a result of the new school which Lalkiamlova established, the education of blind people in Mizoram became a recognised part of government policy. Some of his former students are now working in the government Of course, he took the opportunity to speak to them about the Lord Jesus, who made the blind to see and enabled those with eyes and ears to respond to the good news.

A later appointment allowed Lalkiamlova to develop the concept of self-supported evangelism. Instead of corps and outposts depending on funding from central sources they would find ways of enabling the church to grow within the resources of its own community. Building on his own pioneer experience as a young man he saw many more such schemes develop until now more than 300 evangelists are involved in outreach work, supporting themselves and helped by the sacrificial giving of local sponsors of the work.

Salvationists from Mizoram are now working not only in their own and neighbouring states but also in Sikkim and Arunchal Pradesh, and are exploring the possibilities of work in Nepal. In many ways this has been the most important work accomplished over the years. Who can tell what its ultimate results will be?

During Lalkiamlova's period as the divisional commander in the capital of Mizoram the division become self–financing, 50 missionaries were sponsored and sent out, four new corps and eight societies opened, 1,653 soldiers were made and nine new buildings established. No wonder the soldiers marked his farewell with the gift of a Bible in which these achievements are marked.

Later he was to serve in other Indian territories, where the language and customs were very different from his homeland. He is now convinced that it was right for Mizoram to remain a part of the nation of India. It means that missionaries from his land have the opportunity to preach the gospel in other parts of the nation where it is no longer possible for expatriots to enter.

This boy from a poor home was forced to leave school after only the seventh grade. All education was stopped because of the insurgency. Now he has completed two degree courses, has become a recognised expert in the education of the blind and the author of 10 influential Bible study books.

In 2004 (by then commissioners) he and his wife Puii became zonal leaders at International Headquarters, representing the General in guiding Army work throughout South Asia. Lalkiamlova believes that, with proper guidance, The Salvation Army in Mizoram can become a model for the true spirit of evangelism, self-support and lay ministry that will help to win the world for Jesus Christ.

Back in his home village, the corps now has a new prayer hall on a different site. But at the spot where the old hall stood, on the very highest hill in the village, they have made a new mercy seat out of concrete. Inscribed on it are the same words as on the one in the old hall. It marks the place where the young Lalkiamlova knelt as a young man. Here he realised that you could not save the world with guns and fear. He came to see that it was the love of God, shown first in the sacrifice of Jesus Christ and then demonstrated through his faithful servants, which could change the world.

There are thousands of people in India and now around the world who have found their lives transformed through the ministry of Lalkiamlova and his wife, Lalhlimpuii.

Betty Muleya

THE AFRICAN WOMAN'S CHAMPION

THE AFRICAN WOMAN'S CHAMPION
The story of Betty Muleya

THE place is Sunbury Court Conference Centre where The Salvation Army elects its Generals. The occasion is a meeting of leaders responsible for the Army's development work. The next speaker to mount the podium is a middle-aged Zambian woman with an engaging smile. Her subject is the impact of the HIV/Aids pandemic on the women of her homeland. Her name is Betty Muleya. She works as the co-ordinator of the Aids education programme in her territory.

She tells the story as though it is her own. Here is a young widow, her husband already killed by the virus, who walks miles to the market to sell her vegetables so that her children can have food and she can pay their school fees. Here is an ageing grandmother who has had to take responsibility for her orphaned grandchildren. Here are local Salvationists who have been persuaded to take action to prevent the spread of the disease in their community. Here are village headmen who are willing to change long-held practices to halt the spread of infection.

As Betty speaks it becomes obvious to the conference that she is an expert in her subject. She has done the research. She knows the issues that need to be dealt with. But alongside her expertise is a deep, passionate concern for her people. For Betty, this is a campaign for which she would give her life. If they are given the help they need, the poor women of Africa will find answers to their many problems. They need a champion and Betty will be that champion.

39

It is her personality as much as her knowledge that commends her to the conference. Despite the seriousness of her subject there is a vitality, an optimism, an attractiveness about Betty which communicates itself to her listeners. Those who know her best are aware that it is this same vitality and optimism that has transformed the lives of those with whom she works back home.

Betty is the second-born daughter of long-serving Zambian Salvation Army officers. Majors Andrew and Nelia Muleya were serving in Rhodesia (now Zimbabwe) in 1945 when she was born and Betty was to spend her first 20 years in that country. It is the proud tradition of Salvation Army officers that they share the conditions in which their people live. So Betty lived in simple village houses with primitive conditions and a basic lifestyle. The family grew as a further 10 children were born to their parents.

As one of the older children Betty became a second mother to many of her siblings. She shared the many chores that needed to be done around the home. She was left in charge when Mum and Dad had to attend meetings and conferences. She bought clothes and shoes for the younger ones when she began to work. She helped with their educational fees when she could. None of the younger ones were allowed to suffer if Betty could help. When Nelia Mubeya was promoted to Glory Betty took over many more of her mother's responsibilities at the same time as completing her schooling. Her brother Clement says she was an inspiring figure to all the family. She reconciled family differences and her house became the family's meeting place.

Naturally Betty went to the Army with her parents and the other children. Her mother and father were an inspiration to her. She heard her father preach and shared in the family prayers that were an important and regular part of their family life. It was a vital moment when the faith of the family became her own personal faith and she accepted Jesus Christ as her Saviour and Lord. The spirit of Jesus, his care and concern for others, became part of her nature and she began to find ways of expressing this spirit in her daily life.

Nineteen sixty-five was an important year for Betty. The family were to return to their homeland in the year that it gained its independence as Zambia. Hopes for the future were high in this brand-new country. Betty had gained a place at the David Livingstone Teacher Training College. As she prepared for a career as a teacher, this dynamic young woman seemed to excel in every activity. She became the captain of the college's successful netball team, travelling to matches throughout the country. She was the leader of a dancing team, winning awards and prizes whenever it competed.

After her graduation Betty became a primary school teacher. Her warm personality soon meant that the children in her class came to love her. She knew them all and often went the extra mile to help them with their work. The system required her to move occasionally from one school to another. Head teachers and children were always sorry when Betty had to move on.

Not content with the demands of her school work, Betty took on responsibilities as a Salvation Army soldier. She served as young people's sergeant-major and home league secretary at her home corps. She was a member of the Territorial Songster Brigade. In her spare time she worked as a part-time radio broadcaster, presenting music programmes for patients in hospital.

After a number of years Betty left her work as a school teacher, first to become a social worker and Secretary to the Zambia Blind and Handicapped Society and then to join the Zambia State Insurance Corporation. Here she developed management skills and rose to an important management position in the company. Despite her promotion she still retained the simplicity of lifestyle that she had learned in her parents' home. When her father became unable to look after himself it was Betty who invited him to come and live with her, resigning her position to care for him. She showered her love upon him in his declining years. It was her nature to care.

While she was working at the Insurance Corporation something happened that changed Betty's life. Her brother David was a

Salvation Army officer and his daughter Reginah was staying with Betty while working as a pre-school teacher. Betty began to notice that Reginah was frequently unwell.

HIV infection was already well known in Zambia but Christian families had always assumed that this was not a problem they would have to face. Although Reginah was never tested for HIV infection it became clear to Betty that this was the cause of her illness. No longer could Betty ignore the realities of the spread of this modern-day plague. She spoke to her family about the need to remain faithful to their marriage partners. This was a taboo subject and Betty, a single woman, bravely ignored the customs of her people in tackling this difficult matter.

So Betty, the teacher, now became the nurse. Having taken early retirement she devoted herself to caring for her niece. As she saw Reginah's health deteriorate Betty determined to know more about the disease and how it could be prevented. She made contact with Dr Ian Campbell, who was transforming the hospital at Chikankata into a centre dedicated to the treatment and prevention of Aids. She took training with a counselling service to enable her to help those who were affected by the disease. Loving care and increasing knowledge made Reginah's life more tolerable but it could not prevent her eventual death.

What would Betty do now? She offered her skills in management and teaching, her capacity to care for others and her knowledge of the needs of her people to The Salvation Army. Her first position was as Child Sponsorship and Relief Secretary for Zambia. When famine affected the Siavonga district Betty was involved in a programme to distribute maize to the hungry people. Many children were found sponsors who provided for their education.

But increasingly Betty felt she must devote her time and energy to the crisis that was caused by the rapid spread of HIV infection. She attended a meeting with the Roman Catholic congregation in the district of Libala where she lived. This convinced her that the

Army should be responding more actively. Detailed study and the help of colleagues at Chikankata allowed Betty to begin giving educational talks to people in her own corps and in two other corps nearby.

Many barriers had to be broken down. People were ignorant of the true causes of HIV infection. Those who understood were ashamed if members of their family or their church had become infected. Those coping with HIV were isolated and rejected. Still the numbers of those with the disease grew. The whole community was affected. The people, the church, the corps had to change. They could no longer afford to pretend that there was no HIV. They had to recognise and come to terms with the disease. They must discover how to deal with it.

Some of the most difficult barriers were ancient cultural traditions. These brought strength to the extended family but also threatened to widen the spread of the virus. The widow of a man who had died from HIV infection would become part of the close family of his brother and so could spread the virus to her brother-in-law.

All this increased the burden being borne by poor African women. They had to find the money for the family's needs. It was their task to care for the children. At the same time they had to cope with the illnesses that came with the virus. Worst of all was the anxiety they felt for the future of their family.

Betty had to win the support of key leaders in the community if these attitudes were to change. At first she worked alone and often had to return time and again to communities where the message had not been understood.

One of the leaders in Libala, her home corps, tells the story:

'We never thought of doing it, but through Betty we learned about HIV. After the first workshop we forgot, but she came back again, asking, "What are you doing?" So for a while if she came round we would go the other way and pretend not to see her. Then there was another workshop, and we saw friends doing something in the

43

villages. We reported back to our corps officer and asked for a piece of land. We started a small garden. Then we learned that there were orphans and people who were being neglected. Now we are helping 15 orphans in Grades 1 to 7 and seven in secondary school. The little money we make from the garden goes to pay the school fees.'

Soon Betty's work with HIV had become so important that her leaders decided to create a new position and to make her the co-ordinator for HIV work throughout Zambia. She threw herself into this new task. More and more centres were visited and then, as the workload increased, she found and persuaded other volunteers to act as facilitators for the programme in the areas where they lived. Within three years they were supporting about 1,000 clients in five regions of the country.

Betty's passionate persuasive powers, her non-stop energy, her infectious optimism and her fierce championing of the cause of the women began to make an impact on the people of Zambia.

She constantly journeyed around the remote villages and sprawling townships of Zambia. It would take more than one visit to persuade the elders to make changes in their way of life. She made her way through the bush to a village community for a workshop, then stayed overnight in a rough hut, often without electricity, running water or sewerage. The next day she moved on to another place to continue the work of persuasion and encouragement. At the end of each hectic tour she made her way back to the office to follow up all the work that had been done and to encourage her growing band of facilitators.

On one occasion one of the facilitators made arrangements for a workshop in a remote village location. The headman of the village was very reluctant to attend. 'Is Mbuya coming?' he demanded. (Mbuya means 'grandmother' – the affectionate and respectful name that had been given to Betty by the people.)

'If Mbuya is coming, then we will attend.' Another long journey and visit for Mbuya and another village helped to face the reality of their situation.

Throughout the country small, local schemes of practical help for the victims of HIV – the orphans, the widows, the carers as well as those suffering directly from the effects of the virus – began to develop. Betty's drive, enthusiasm and knowledge were beginning to be recognised. Other groups in Zambia and internationally began to ask for her advice. She visited Kenya, Malawi, Zimbabwe and Uganda to speak about her work and to encourage others to begin similar schemes. She was invited to Canada and Britain to be a speaker at important conferences on development issues.

With all this recognition and appreciation Betty remained the simple, unspoiled champion of the poor. Treated to a large portion of fried fish and chips on a London visit, Betty could not eat all the meal. She carefully wrapped the remaining food and ate it cold for breakfast next morning. There was no way that she would waste food by throwing it away!

Despite her important contribution to the work of her country she insisted on living a very simple life. She had been brought up in an officer's quarters and continued to live in that plain style. Her home on a compound in Lusaka was called 'Nakeempa' by the family. It reminded them of the remote village where her grandfather had been born. It was a place of refuge, a place to seek advice and help for all the family. They were always welcome there on the occasions when Betty was at home. It was a reminder of where they had come from.

One day, at the headquarters building in Lusaka, Lieut-Colonel Geoff Blurton, who was then the Chief Secretary for Zambia, heard a knock at his office door. It was Betty. She closed the door carefully and sat down. Her usually cheerful face was serious. 'I have some bad news to share,' she said.

'My doctor tells me that I have breast cancer. I have been putting off an appointment for some time because I have been so busy. Now he tells me that he cannot offer any treatment.'

The colonel was devastated. Betty's work was so important. No one could replace her. But the anxiety that he felt was much more

45

for the suffering of a friend and colleague. Betty's dynamic personality had made such an impact that the thought of her serious illness seemed like a tragedy.

Every effort was made to find help for Betty. The finest hospital treatment in South Africa was arranged. Support from her many friends and family was offered. But the cancer was too advanced. Betty had been so busy caring for others that she had neglected herself. She was so consumed by her campaign for the people of Zambia that her own health seemed to be unimportant.

In her final weeks she spent time with her brother Clement, who was also very sick. Encouraging him to trust in the Lord, she pointed him to the Saviour in whom she never failed to trust. 'Precious in the sight of the Lord is the death of his saints' (Psalm 116:15) was a favourite verse that was a great encouragement to her.

What was it that gave Betty the power to change the habits and traditions of her people? What authority did she have to talk to elders and headmen about their behaviour? How could she persuade The Salvation Army that HIV/Aids was their problem and not something that could be hidden away?

It was her integrity as a Christian and a Salvationist. It was her passionate concern for others. It was her single-minded determination to confront issues that others wanted to ignore. It was her willingness to give herself to a task that was bigger than her own health and happiness. In the end she gave her life for her people. That was the spirit of Jesus Christ in Mbuya – Betty Muleya of Zambia.

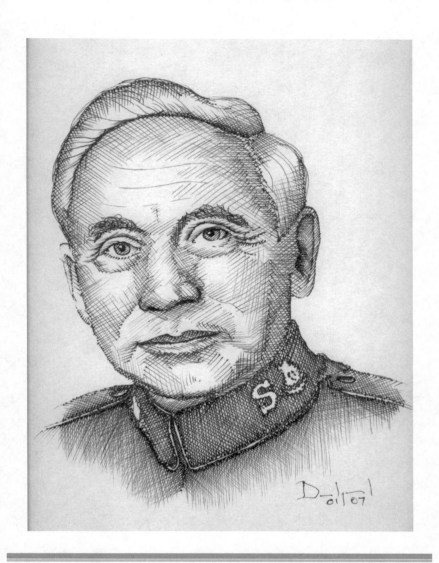

Harry Williams

THE SURGEON

THE SURGEON
The story of Commissioner (Dr) Harry Williams, OBE, OF

'DOCTOR, look at my hands. I have no feeling in my fingers. I cannot even pick up a stone. I will never be able to do my work as a farmer.' The English doctor recognised the clear signs of leprosy. His young Indian patient faced the fear of his friends as well as the consequences of his disease. 'I can help you,' said the doctor. 'It will take a little while and careful surgery but I can remake your hands. Then we will teach you a new trade so that you can remake your life.'

Many years later the foreman of the rehabilitation workshop at Catherine Booth Hospital, Nagercoil, India, greeted the returning doctor by showing him his hands. The tiny white scars from the operations, the flexible fingers and his important position in the unit were the evidence that the promise of a new life had been fulfilled.

The next patient was a middle-aged woman. When she removed the scarf veiling her face there was a hole where the nose should have been. An angry, jealous husband had attacked her years before. Now she had heard of the doctor who could rebuild faces. 'Can you help me?' 'Yes, of course,' was the reply. It would take all his professional knowledge, all his craftsman's skill, all his artistry and the compassion of a Christian missionary to do the work. But the face would be remade and the woman's dignity restored.

Who was this expert plastic surgeon working in the heat of southern India?

What was his motivation? How did he maintain the hectic pace that he always set himself?

Harry Williams was born into a comfortable home in a London suburb. The year was 1913. His father worked in the financial heart of the city. The family went to a large Salvation Army corps and, as a teenager, Harry took part in all the activities there. He was an intelligent young man, excelling at science and crafts. He had artistic gifts that found expression in painting. He thought he would join his father in the city and live very pleasantly.

But the Holy Spirit was at work in his life. Perhaps it was through the ministry from the platform or the influence of godly friends and mentors at the corps. By the time he was 17 Harry had found a personal saviour in Jesus Christ and determined that his life must be spent helping others. He would study medicine. He would push himself hard to achieve the highest goals.

When he passed his first medical examination, his friends at the corps were delighted. 'If you are going to be a doctor you should let the Army leaders know,' said one and arranged for him to have tea with Colonel (Dr) Percy Turner, the Army's Chief Medical Officer. Within two days an interview at International Headquarters was planned.

'Doctors have been a lot of trouble to the Army,' grumbled the commissioner conducting the interview. But he was pleased enough with Harry and before the end of the interview the young man had signed papers and was soon to be on his way to the International Training College.

When he reflected on the experience much later in life, it seemed to Harry that this was just like being pressed into service as a sailor! But it was said with a twinkle in his eye. He never regretted the suddenness of the decision. It shaped the whole of the rest of his life.

After commissioning came continued medical studies, qualification as a physician, and courtship with Eileen Neeve, who was a nurse and a candidate for officership. When Eileen became an officer they were quickly married and set sail for India. It was to be their place of work for 30 years.

From the earliest days of the Army's work in India there had been a desire to be involved in a healing ministry. The beginnings were simple, well-meaning and amateur. The Christian churches of India provided medical care for the people, especially for the poor. They saw it as a way to express their love for Christ and his people. It soon became clear that greater expertise and professional standards would be needed. Dr Percy Turner, Harry's mentor, had led the way and other distinguished doctors had followed.

The first appointment for Harry and Eileen was to the Thomas Emery Hospital in Moradabad, where Harry was the assistant to Dr Edgar Stevens, an expert surgeon who was the son of a pioneer Salvation Army missionary. There was much to learn about living in a new country and practising medicine in less than ideal conditions. It was the time of the Second World War and the workload increased as war casualties had to be treated alongside the local community. The hospital was requisitioned by the military authorities and Harry served as a medical military officer in Poona, being graded as a surgeon.

During this time Eileen and Harry knew profound sorrow that came with the death of their eldest daughter, Ann. It was a medical accident and the parents, doctors and nurses themselves felt it keenly. Anne's grave in Poona marks the Williams's loss and the price of their service in India.

The hard work needed to go on and a brief holiday in Britain allowed Harry to gain higher surgical qualifications at Edinburgh University. On their return to India they were appointed to lead the hospital at Dhariwal in the Punjab.

Here they served the medical needs of a large local factory. The extra income this brought enabled them to offer care to the many poor people in the surrounding area and to commence the training of nurses.

Harry always wanted to use his skills in the way that was most useful to the community. This meant being willing to adapt the work of the hospital to the changing needs. A big change happened in India at this time. The British rulers left and the great Indian nation became independent. For a time there was chaos as Hindus and Muslims moved in their millions between the new countries of India and Pakistan. Violence erupted and Christian missionaries might have felt their lives were endangered.

Harry and Eileen and their little family worked through the troubles, offering care and healing to everyone whatever their religion or politics. They were encouraged by the local Indian Salvationists, who took no part in the violence but simply rolled up their sleeves and offered practical help to their neighbours.

Life for a surgeon at a Salvation Army hospital was always busy and often exciting. Both at Dhariwal and at their next appointment at Anand in Western India, the Williams family coped with the unending stream of patients needing help. Deep x-ray equipment was installed by Harry and Ken Tutton, who had experience as a radiographer.

Visits to outlying hospitals and to remote villages where there was no doctor meant long and difficult journeys over dangerous Himalayan roads. Sometimes the whole family went, when daughters Jennifer and Fleur were not at their boarding school miles away from home.

No officers expect to be rich, but these years proved to be very hard for the family. Any money raised by the use of Harry's professional skill went into the hospital funds. He took the basic allowance for an officer and the family lived as simply as their Indian neighbours.

Harry met a colleague with whom he had trained as a doctor. Dr Paul Brand had become an expert in the treatment of bones and joints and now was concerned with the problems of leprosy. This ancient disease, often mentioned in the Bible, caused so much distress because the symptoms were clearly seen. Hands and feet became useless and faces shapeless and ugly. Many people thought the disease was easily caught, even though this was not true, so people with leprosy were thrown out of their homes and villages and had to live like outcasts.

Dr Brand believed that the new science of plastic surgery could help many who suffered from leprosy. In England this new work had been pioneered by Sir Archibald McIndoe. He helped many soldiers and airmen who had been badly burned in the war. Harry Williams determined to learn this new skill. He had the opportunity to help 10 lepers from a Government hospital in Ahmadabad. They desperately wanted Harry to give them new noses. How happy they were with the results of these first operations!

On his next furlough in England Harry took the opportunity to learn more of the new skills when he worked under Sir Archibald. Returning to India as the head of the largest Salvation Army hospital at Nagercoil, he was determined to introduce his new programme to the hospital. The nurses and the other patients were horrified. Harry had always worked closely with the nursing staff and admired their care and compassion. But this time they went on strike. They would not care for lepers. They were sure they would catch the disease and suffer just like the patients. Harry, Eileen and their small team of missionary nurses took over the care of the wards for 24 hours a day.

Then, in the Sunday morning worship meeting at the hospital one of the Christian nurses came forward to the mercy seat. She laid her doubts and fears before the Lord and led her colleagues back to work. The outstanding professional care and compassion that the nurses gave to their patients was a major part of the healing process offered to those with this dreaded disease. Because of the high standards of the hospital none of the staff ever became a victim. Leprosy was not a disease to be feared like a plague but it required skill and love to deal with its effects.

Catherine Booth Hospital at Nagercoil had long been known as a centre of excellence. It had established a training school for nurses and doctors. Locally trained people were able to add to the skills of those who had come from overseas and a very high standard of care was offered.

Alongside the medical work at the hospital Harry established units to help the patients to recover. They needed to rebuild muscles and to learn to work at new trades. Equipment was needed to enable those who had lost limbs to walk. A workshop was set up to make this equipment. All this extra work needed skilled supervision. It was part of the healing process.

Most important of all was the healing of the spirit. Doctors, nurses and patients were all invited to be part of the hospital's spiritual programme.

The hospital had the largest corps in the territory and the medical staff had a wonderful ministry. Harry has spoken of the atmosphere that existed: 'Gentleness, compassion and an infectious confidence in God ... awakens patients to that fullness of life of which physical recovery is only a part.'

All through the 30 years of his service in India, Harry Williams brought together the skills of a surgeon with the commitment of a Christian missionary.

He served the Indian people not only because they were in need of his special gifts but also because they were souls for whom Jesus Christ died. His own love of Christ demanded that he cared for them.

Captain (Dr) Hazel Scott, one of Harry's team at Nagercoil, found a three-year-old girl in a nearby village. One leg and foot had been infected and was four times the size of the other. Sosamma had never walked. She was brought to the hospital and Harry operated on her leg. The operation was successful. Within three weeks Sosamma was running about the hospital compound completely well.

One day Harry received a call from the Governor of Kerala Province. (He would later become the President of India). Would the doctor please call at the Governor's Palace? A large limousine was sent for Harry. The governor's wife had a serious facial problem. An urgent operation was needed to repair her damaged nose. The hospital had to set aside a nursing home for their distinguished patient and her entourage. The problem was resolved. When the governor spoke at an All-India Conference of Ministers of Health he paid tribute to the work of the Army hospital. He said:

'Recently I visited the Catherine Booth Hospital at Nagercoil. This hospital run by The Salvation Army has nearly 400 beds. From outside it looks small, housed in modest buildings in a limited area. Surprisingly the hospital is one of the best in the country, with experts attending patients, and the cleanliness is something that every hospital should emulate. This only shows that the lack of finances or limited resources need not stand in the way of having a good hospital.'

The High Commissioner for the United Kingdom was so impressed with Harry's development of plastic surgery to meet the needs of sufferers from leprosy that he recommended that he should be made an Officer of the Order of the British Empire. The British Queen gave him this honour.

The Christian Medical Association of India was very concerned about the victims of the war which was raging in Vietnam at this time. Harry agreed to treat Vietnamese children who had suffered from terrible burns in his Indian hospital. Sadly the Government of Vietnam would not allow them to leave the country so Harry, along with a group of British specialist surgeons, agreed to rotate in short-term assignments in Vietnam itself.

He often had to go to pick up patients by small military aircraft. This was very risky and he frequently found himself under fire. They came across one patient whose legs had been fused together by a firebomb. Intricate, delicate surgery took skin from other undamaged places and separated the legs, restoring full movement and health.

For the final hospital appointment Harry and Eileen had been separated from their family. Their two daughters had returned to England to complete their education. Harry and Eileen were not able to return home for their daughters' weddings and missed special family occasions. But when the General suggested that Harry should leave his surgical work to become the leader of the Army in south India they agreed to this appointment still far from home.

Next came appointments to New Zealand and Australia. Harry combined his leadership of the Army in those countries with work to promote and regulate medicine. His long experience and recognised skill were widely appreciated.

Part of his responsibility in Australia was for pioneering the Army in Papua New Guinea. This very undeveloped country was about to be made independent. There were scarcely any medical resources outside of its capital Port Moresby. What could The Salvation Army do to help?

All Harry's training and experience meant that he wanted to establish a high-quality professional hospital service. But there were no doctors available and no elaborate buildings in the remote highland areas. Many villages were asking the Army to send preachers and carers.

Harry devised a scheme. If the village would supply a young Christian convert and a simple building for a community centre, the Army would train the volunteer as preacher and medical man. So young men, trained in sharing the gospel and in spotting the most frequent diseases, went into these remote areas. They carried a basic kit of simple drugs and knew how to deal with common problems. They would return for more training and guidance and soon transformed their communities. The gospel and good health were brought to many thousands of people.

It was not surprising that the Army needed Harry's knowledge and experience in its top international leadership team. He and Eileen returned to London to a wide variety of responsibilities.

These included planning the development of medical work, oversighting the work in the Americas, representing the Army at the World Council of Churches and even deciding what music should be published.

Harry had never visited South America but he wanted to understand its particular needs to plan for the future of Army work there. He visited Bolivia, where an enthusiastic local leader had many plans for growth. The country's second city of Cochabamba was surrounded by many crowded slums. The Army had no work there and there was great need.

An officer-couple came from Sweden. The Swedish government gave a grant. A nurse came from England. Enthusiastic support from the local people established a community centre. This then became a clinic and a small hospital. It was named 'The Harry Williams Hospital'. When Harry retired from active service he was proud of what had been achieved there. But 10 years later, at the age of 79, he heard disturbing news. Local non-salvationist leadership had changed the hospital. It was now being run for their personal profit.

Harry gathered together his medical equipment, including his plastic surgery tools and left his retirement home in England. He went to live and work again in the high mountains of Bolivia. All his skills as doctor, surgeon, leader and negotiator were needed to put things right at Cochabamba. For some months he battled with the problems and in the end they were resolved. In thankfulness this basic hospital caring for thousands of poor slum-dwellers honoured Commissioner Williams at its silver jubilee in 2004.

All his life Harry has known change and has learned to adapt to all the new circumstances that surrounded him. At the age of 90 he mourned the loss of his lifetime's partner when Eileen was promoted to Glory. He then moved from rural Norfolk to live close to his daughter in Scotland. He still paints and sells his pictures to support the work at Cochabamba.

Looking back on a life that has been full of surprises, he can trace the work of the Holy Spirit in his life. From that first awareness of the need to serve others as a doctor, through all the adaptations to meet the needs of people, through countless adventures and dangers, the Lord has been with him.

The Salvation Army, which has provided the way for him to serve, admitted Commissioner Williams to its highest honour for distinguished service, the Order of the Founder, in 2005. He gives all the glory to God.

Kathryn Cox

THE PRISON MINISTER

60

THE PRISON MINISTER
The story of Kathryn Cox

'DON'T preach to me!' said the angry young man. 'How do you expect me to get rid of my anger? I only have 28 days to live.' He was talking to Major Kathryn Cox as he waited in Texas, at the largest 'Death Row' in the world for his execution. Kathryn admitted that she could not deal with his fury but she knew someone who could. The half-Apache Indian, half-Spanish young man had asked her to be his spiritual adviser. He was angry because no one had been able to find his mother or any other member of his family. He did not want to die without seeing them again.

The next day Kathryn visited his mother, who was seriously ill with kidney failure, and within a week the young man had been visited by his father, two brothers and two sisters. The condemned man broke down in his cell seeking forgiveness for all his past. Then Kathryn found his daughter, a 12-year-old whom he had not seen since his conviction 11 years earlier. The girl spent the last four days of her father's life with him as he prepared in peace for his life's ending. 'What a time that was!' said Kathy as she remembered the overwhelming emotions of that experience.

Kathryn Cox is driven by a concern for other people that is compulsive. It probably came from her childhood experiences. Unlike the wealthy sophisticated cities of North America, in which she has worked, she was born in one of the small rural mountain communities of West Virginia in 1924. During the Great Depression of the 1930s these communities were desperately poor. Many of the coal mines were closed, banks failed and those industries that retained their workers paid very low wages. Hunger was seen on the faces of almost every family. Stories are told of children dying because no milk or flour was available.

Kathryn was one of eight children in a poor family. Her mother brought up her children to have a simple and trusting Christian faith. She taught them that they should never be ashamed of being poor. But they were often hungry and lived on the most basic of foods. Young Kathryn became aware of family tragedy when two members of her close family were killed. The grief that the family went through at this time must have made an impact on Kathryn's young heart. She might have given way to despair and hopelessness, finding relief in alcohol or drugs. Instead she seemed to find an understanding of the sufferings of other people that would become her life's motivation.

Two of her sisters became alcoholics while Kathryn was still a small child. One day, sister Eloise ran away from home. Mother searched for her for days going from bar to bar, eventually fainting in the street from hunger and anxiety. The police took her to The Salvation Army. The local corps officer – Captain Kenneth Moss – found the missing sister and reunited the family.

So The Salvation Army came into young Kathy's life in a dramatic way. She attended the little corps that met in a store-front hall. At the age of nine she knelt at the mercy seat there. The words on the penitent form read: 'Here bring your wounded hearts'. Kathy's young heart had been wounded. She would suffer many more wounds over the years but on that day she found the Saviour who can heal wounds and restore to mental, physical and spiritual health.

From the beginning she knew she must spend her life caring for others. She wanted to point others to the One who could mend their wounded hearts.

It seemed natural that this would be through officership in the Army. So for Kathy conversion and calling came together. She would become a servant of the Master who had brought her freedom and release.

Kathryn entered the training college in 1943 and has served as an officer for 63 years. For many of those years her ministry was shared with Major Kimber Cox whom she married the year after her commissioning. They served as corps officers and found great joy in this ministry. It was when her husband was appointed to a correctional services ministry that Kathryn began to take a special interest in this work. She had always found fulfilment in compassionate pastoral ministry. It was a gift that God had given to her. She could see good in even the worst of people and profoundly believed that they could be changed by the Holy Spirit's power.

Kathryn Cox became a spiritual adviser to Texas prisons in 1986. At the age of 83 she still continues her ministry. She sees herself as an honoured guest in this place of punishment. 'Death Row' is a city of about 500 people. They live in separate cells and are locked in for 23 hours each day. The atmosphere is always emotional, for the inhabitants of this city have to think about the end of their lives. The tensions that surround the long judicial process are huge. Men and women may spend many years not knowing when their case will be finalised and the sentence carried out.

Into this scene of anger, grief, despair and hopelessness Kathryn brings a message of life, hope and peace. She says that those who have accepted Christ as their Saviour now call the place 'Life Row'. It is for them a place of new beginnings as well as of endings.

It was not long before Kathryn realised that this work demanded not only a deep Christian compassion but also a professional level of skill. The opportunity came to add to her gifts through education. A degree in psychology and a master's degree in criminal justice prepared her for the task that would occupy the rest of her life.

Kathryn has a profound belief in the importance of the Bible. She knows that when people study this book they can come to know the Saviour who is its great theme. So from the beginning of her ministry Kathryn has encouraged the inmates of the prisons to take part in correspondence courses based on the Bible. When they write down their answers they begin to understand the truth. She firmly believes that studying the Scriptures and responding in written answers opens the door to the transformation that the Holy Spirit can work in the human heart.

When she visits them, Kathryn persuades the prisoners to undertake the study programme, marks the papers, encourages the students and watches with amazement at the changes in their understanding and personality that occur.

Kathryn offers a Bible study course to all the men and women she deals with. Jim Vanderbilt, an ex-policeman and an inhabitant of Death Row, was one who took up the offer of the courses and later was able to study the New Testament in the original Greek with the help of a lexicon. His conversion was so genuine that Kathy was able to say of him, 'He is a true believer and an example of how the Word of God delivers those on Death Row.' Jim said about his counsellor, supporter and Bible tutor, 'Kathy is God's chosen instrument in my life to help me walk with Christ. We share joys and griefs, defeats and victories; she helps me accept myself as a worthy human being despite the world's rejection. This is the true meaning of love.'

When she started out on this ministry it was with many doubts about her ability to cope with the demands it would make on her. As she looked at the first sets of lessons that came to her desk she felt she was not competent to minister to these people. The digits on the lesson pages showed that these men were about to be executed. Kathryn searched the Scriptures as she prayed for guidance and direction to begin her task. She wanted a special anointing for the work that had been given to her. She found it in words of Psalm 102: 'He will regard the prayer of the destitute and not despise their prayer … To hear the groaning of the prisoner; to loose those that are appointed to death.'

Here was the grace she needed to fulfil her ministry – a ministry that has lasted far beyond the years of her active officership and long into what should have been a leisurely retirement.

Now she spends two full days every week at the prison. One of the most demanding parts of her work is to attend the execution of those whom she has helped and have been condemned to death. Every condemned man has the right to ask for a spiritual adviser to be present when the sentence is carried out. Kathryn has attended 41 executions, often of those she has helped to find the Saviour. These occasions are always deeply moving for her.

'At each execution, God bathes these people and me with a glory in Christ that transforms us. I witness the glory of the coming of the Lord to take them Home. The fact that they allow me to help God usher their souls into eternity is the greatest honour they can bestow upon me. I am blessed,' she writes.

One evening Kathryn was watching the news when she saw a young lawyer sitting next to the newscaster. He had been involved in a long court battle for the custody of his son which he had lost. He had taken a gun into the courtroom. He shot two judges and three lawyers, killing two of them. Then he went straight to the television studio to turn himself in.

Kathryn understood the man's loneliness and his despair and felt deeply for him. He defended himself at the trial and appeal, offering no excuses and accepting the death penalty imposed. Kathryn counselled him and went with him to his death. She is convinced that his death served no purpose and that one of his victims who pleaded for the sentence to be revoked was right. It was the trauma and tragedy of his broken life that had forced him over the edge of sanity.

Some of the people to whom Kathy ministers have come to their present situation because of the use of drugs. One young man had graduated from high school with honours and had not even committed a traffic offence until he was introduced to amphetamines. After five weeks on the drugs he killed two people

65

without provocation. He was tormented by what he had done and Kathy came to talk to him. She mentioned Brahms' music one day and watched as he played out the lullaby with his fingers on the counter between them. She sang to him Catherine Baird's words set to the melody:

> *Let your heart be at rest for life's pathway runs steep,*
> *And with death there's a tryst that the body must keep.*
> *Though the future be veiled, thou shalt not be afraid,*
> *For the peace of the Lord on thy heart has been laid.*

It was the turning point for the young man. As they executed him he was singing: 'Because he lives, I can face tomorrow. Because he lives, all fear is gone.'

Kathryn received this letter from an inmate with whom she was corresponding. It was a confirmation of the importance of the work she was doing. He wrote: 'Revenge! All I wanted was revenge – revenge for what I felt my wife had done to me. In one terrible moment my love turned to hate, a hate so fierce it literally robbed me of my sanity, blinded me to reason. The next hours are too terrible to tell, but as I groped my way out of the fog that had enveloped me, four of my five children were dead. I was their murderer!

'When I gave myself up, they took me to a hospital and tried to help me, but the only way they could block out my torment for what I had done was to put me to sleep with drugs. My remorse, my agony over the death of my children by my hand, made life a pure hell.

'Under the devastation of my ordeal which left its deep and permanent traces, I am aware that I have been touched by a new dimension of reality. The power of God's Spirit penetrated the centre of my mental illness. Now I have become a better person and have become deeply alive in Christ. I am a man tied permanently to imprisonment, yet through resurrection, I have risen above the confines of my situation.'

Kathryn cares passionately for those she seeks to counsel. She sees an intensity in their lives for every moment is precious. Locked in a cell with no window, every detail takes on an exaggerated meaning. The sense of isolation is overwhelming.

She hates injustice and believes that the death penalty is the greatest injustice of all. It costs far more to pay for all the legal costs surrounding the death penalty than it would to keep a man in prison. She has built a strong relationship with other church agencies to help the men continue their non-violent opposition to this punishment. Nevertheless while Death Row exists she continues to help the people who have to endure its horrors. She is convinced that the one hope for those who have to live on the edge of despair is found in an acceptance of Jesus as Saviour and the peace of heart that this knowledge gives to them.

'I had expected to see men devoid of hope, dejected, bitter, angry and dangerous,' she said, 'but most of them have long since cultivated life in Christ. I had been told that convicts distrust everyone. Wrong! I had been told for years that all convicted men and women say they're innocent. Wrong! Far more people have begged to tell me what they did.'

She encourages such confession, not that it is necessary for her to hear the story, but because the truth sets people free. She even says that she has found more loyalty, respect and honesty on Death Row than among professionals and even those in spiritual ministry.

Her Death Row converts often say that Christ was executed rather than saying that he was crucified. This helps them to identify with the One who shared their lot.

Such work is costly. Kathryn pays a heavy price for the loving care she offers.

She speaks of the overwhelming sorrow that comes to her as she sees the eyes of the many men and women she has accompanied to the execution chamber. She feels deeply for the families both of the victims of the crimes and the perpetrators. The only relief for such pain is her own relationship with Jesus Christ, her Saviour and theirs. At times Kathryn knows the depths of human despair. She has to live with this intensity of emotion but it produces a kind of caring that reaches out to others who know the same feelings.

In the times of great elation Kathryn still shows enormous energy and drive. She is driven by a compulsion to share her knowledge of the Saviour. She is in her office by 5.30 each morning. She keeps a file card of each prisoner who is on her study programme. At the moment she has over 62,000 active members. She knows which prison every man is in. She has marked well over a million Bible lesson papers. Even in the moments of her greatest despair she finds relief in her work of encouragement and challenge with her correspondents.

It is not surprising that many of the prison staff value her work so highly. One prison warden said he wished he had 500 Kathryn Coxes to work in his prison. Her intelligence and passionate commitment to her task are shared with everyone who meets her.

What is it that keeps her going? What is her motivation? Kathryn replies:

'Death Row does not need to be a tomb. Through the penetration of the Word, it can be a great womb stirring to life the beginnings if a myriad of miracles. Always the mystery, the miracle, the meaning and the ministry of the Resurrection through the Word!'

Through her own tireless ministry she has become a midwife into the new life of the Kingdom of God for many who otherwise would have died in hopeless despair.

Alida Bosshardt

THE PROSTITUTES' FRIEND

THE PROSTITUTES' FRIEND
The story of Alida Bosshardt

'FATHER, I hate school,' said 14-year-old Alida Bosshardt. 'I want to find a job that will let me meet people.' Mr Bosshardt was anxious for his daughter. It was not easy to find work in Holland in 1927. His own grocery business had failed. He thought she would need all the schooling she could get if she was to succeed. Life at school was hard. They laughed at her because she went to the Roman Catholic church. But Alida was determined. She would show them that she could make her own way in the world. Soon she persuaded her father and went to work as a shop assistant in the Dutch city of Utrecht. She was popular with both her customers and her employer.

Living in the Bosshardt home was complicated. Father had become a Roman Catholic, Mother was a member of the Dutch Reformed Church. Alida and her adopted brother went to both churches but found no inspiration. They did not understand the Catholic services in Latin and the long sermons in the Dutch church went over their heads.

Then one day her brother told Alida that a brass band was holding open-air services in the town square. It was The Salvation Army. Alida went to listen and followed the Salvationists to their hall. Here, in simple language, she learned that Jesus loved her and that she could find forgiveness and peace through him. She accepted Jesus as her saviour and gradually became more involved in the work of the Army.

Her father was unhappy that Alida was going to the Army. He thought an interview with the bishop would soon put a stop to this nonsense. The bishop told her that Salvationists were good at washing people's faces but the church was more concerned with washing their souls. Alida told the story of her conversion and what she was doing. When she finally emerged from the interview it was with a donation from the bishop for the work of the Army.

The great day came when Alida was enrolled as a Salvation Army soldier. She was proud of her uniform but aware that everyone now would know she belonged to the Army. Soon after this she began working at an Army children's home and giving her spare time at the corps. She had found the direction for her life and that direction was never to change.

She applied to enter training and become an officer. The Army authorities were not so sure! They thought her health was not good. Would it stand up to the hard work of an officer? Was her education sufficient to do the work? They thought Alida was a serious risk. If she failed in the first five years she would have to go back home. Her father had to guarantee that he would accept her back.

Life at the training college was not easy for Alida. She had a mind of her own. She was more interested in practical matters than in complicated theological discussion. She even failed an examination and wondered if they would send her away. But the college officers saw some special qualities in this young woman. They saw her determination, her single-minded concentration on the work and her love for people.

Soon Lieutenant Bosshardt was appointed to assist at the Rotterdam corps and, one year later, she was delighted to be appointed to the children's home. This was just the work she wanted. It meant long hours and required great patience, but she loved the children and they loved her in return. She had found the way to serve God by loving the people who needed her most.

This was a difficult time in The Netherlands. The Nazis had come to power in Germany and were persecuting the Jews. Then the Second World War broke out and Holland was invaded. The

Nazi occupiers had no time for The Salvation Army. They saw it as a British organisation and banned it. Dutch Salvationists reluctantly left off their uniforms and met together as Christians wherever and however they could. All the social homes had to sever their connections with the Army.

The children's home where Alida worked was very short of money and soon found that many more children, mostly from Jewish families, were being brought to them. Many of the parents feared deportation and Alida and her colleagues had to find a way of caring for the children. Some came wearing the hated yellow star on their clothes that showed they were Jewish, but Alida quickly decided that in this home there would be no stars and no discrimination.

With little money and many children to care for Alida needed to find funds. She visited farms to beg for food for the home. She went to the markets at the end of the day to ask for unsold food. The authorities accused her of raising money for the forbidden Salvation Army but she told them it was only for the children in the home that she was collecting.

Alida persisted with her collecting but someone betrayed her to the authorities. A German military officer took her to the police station and locked her up in small room. For three days she was questioned but she would not change her story. She told the officer of the work the home was doing and how much her help was needed. Perhaps this officer, who seemed sympathetic, was persuaded by her determined arguments. After three long days Alida was taken back to her cell and, somehow, the authorities forgot to lock the door after her! Alida promptly walked out of the police station and straight back to the children's home.

'You can't stay here. They will arrest all of us,' said her colleagues. So for two weeks Alida lived in a tent in the forest until the trouble died down and she was able to return to her work.

Then one day a military officer came to the home. He demanded that the children leave and requisitioned the house for the use of the German forces. He wanted to look all around the property but Alida was concerned that he would recognise some of the Jewish children and take them away. So she kept him talking in the office while others made arrangements to find a new place for the children to stay. They had to leave the beds but managed to take with them enough blankets to keep the family warm.

Another building was found for the home, and all the children and the helpers walked to their new house. During the five years of the wartime occupation Alida and the children had to move 12 times. Sometimes it was because of bomb damage and other times because of orders from the German authorities. On one occasion there was a very bad raid while the children were being moved and they had to take cover in the basement of the central train station in Amsterdam.

In all the war years none of the children in the care of the home was killed, injured or lost. In recognition of this remarkable work for Jewish families, Alida was honoured with the highest award that the state of Israel can offer to non-Jews. On her 90th birthday she was recognised as 'Righteous Among the Nations' by the Yad Vashem holocaust memorial organisation.

With the ending of the war came a change of work for Captain Bosshardt. Her leaders felt she needed a less stressful task. She was appointed to headquarters to assist the leader of the social work. But Alida did not like working in an office. She longed to be with people who needed her love and care. When people came to the office seeking help it was always Alida who went to deal with them.

In the evenings, when her official work was done she would seek out other people who needed her help. The office was near the 'red light' district in Amsterdam and Alida began to make friends with and offer help to some of the women who worked there. She saw how much they needed both practical and spiritual support and she longed to be able to devote all her time and energy to this work.

So one day Captain Bosshardt made her way to the office of the Army's leader in The Netherlands. 'Please let me do this work full time. I will find a way to meet the costs and a building to work in. All I ask is the freedom to do the work'. The commissioner gave her a small grant, a new flag and prayed with her. He then told her she was now on her own! Alida left the office to start the work for which she would become a legend in her lifetime.

She began in one small basement room which was both her living accommodation and her centre. For many years a small place like this was home for 'the Major', as she became known throughout Amsterdam. For the first 10 years she worked alone, building up contacts and offering sympathetic help to all who approached her. Open-air meetings with a small group of supporters were held every week. Alida's home-cum-office was always open to enable her to counsel those who came to her. When people were refused admission to the hostels for the homeless Alida found them somewhere to stay. Soon she could claim that she knew every one of the 2,000 prostitutes working in the red light district.

She never condemned the lifestyle of the people she sought to help. Although strictly observing the Army's rules about her own life, she saw the prostitutes and their clients as people in need of love and understanding. They soon began to trust this woman who would always tell them the truth and who had no other motive than to offer them help. They saw in her God's love in action.

Alida had promised her leader she would find the money to make her project work. She sold hundreds of copies of *The War Cry* in the bars each week. She persuaded friends to support her work, sending them regular newsletters, all typed on her own old machine.

The work grew and it became obvious that a larger centre was needed to cope with the demands and to house her growing group of volunteer workers. Alida noticed that the oldest brick building in Amsterdam, called *d'Leewenburgh*, was standing empty. It was a famous landmark and belonged to a preservation group in the city. Major Bosshardt went to see the director of the group. At first he would not even consider allowing this precious building to be used for her work. But the major persisted. Eventually the contract was arranged and the goodwill centre was established in its new home. Today it is still at the heart of the work, with a counselling centre, an accommodation area and offices.

The stories of those who have been helped by the goodwill centre would fill many volumes. Men whose addiction to alcohol or drugs had ruined their health and destroyed their relationships drifted into this part of the city. When they made their way to the goodwill centre they found understanding people who offered practical help without condemning them. Young women caught up in prostitution found someone who could enable them to get out of the business. Others who remained in this work found an unchanging friend in the major and kept this friendship over many years. Asylum seekers from every part of the world found kind and helpful support from those working in the centre.

After 10 years of hard but rewarding work Major Bosshardt had a team of well-trained and compassionate assistants, but she remained the inspiring director of the programme. Now she realised that her lack of education and professional skills would hold back the development of the work. So the middle-aged major who had left school at 14 went back to college to study for a degree in social work. She sat alongside students who were young enough to be her children and had to work very hard to catch up with their level of schooling. What a triumphant day it was when she graduated!

By now the work of the goodwill centre was growing far beyond its one-person beginnings. A hostel for women and another for men were established. A corps operated from its own building, for Alida never separated the practical work from the spiritual ministry. Real change in the lives of her people could only be made when Jesus made the difference in their lives. The work was so effective that the Dutch nation began to take note of the wonderful things happening in their capital city. The beautiful but degraded area of which they were somewhat ashamed was being renewed by the work of this simple follower of Jesus Christ.

On 19 February 1959 Dutch television broadcast a version of the *This is your Life* show. Major Bosshardt believed she had been invited to talk about her work to a women's group. Instead she discovered she was to be the star of the show. Initially she was taken aback and not at all pleased that the leader of the Army's social work in The Netherlands knew all about the plan and was sitting in the audience. But, as the story unfolded, and colleagues and clients told about the wonderful support they had received, the major realised that this was an opportunity to share the gospel and to secure the money that the centre needed.

The response to the programme was overwhelming. Offers of goods, money and time came from all over the country. No longer would the centre have to struggle for its funding. Now she could extend the work of the centre to more of Amsterdam's needy people.

The next year saw Major Bosshardt invited to the royal palace for an audience with Queen Juliana. Their long conversation showed how much the monarch appreciated and understood the work being done. The Queen promised her encouragement and support for the goodwill centre. Princess Beatrix (now Queen of The Netherlands) was then a young woman who also showed great interest in Alida's work. She asked if she could come to see the work for herself. Her parents thought it was not wise to do so.

Two years later the same request was sent to the Dutch government, who also vetoed the idea. Finally Princess Beatrix decided she would go anyway. Alida dared not tell her Army leaders about the plan. They could never approve something the Government had turned down.

So one day, disguised in dark glasses and a shawl, the princess arrived at the centre. She went with Major Bosshardt to visit some of the poorest homes in the district. She met some of the prostitutes and asked them why they did this work. She saw the terrible circumstances in which people lived.

Later in the evening she went with Alida to sell *The War Cry* in the bars of the red light district. The disguise worked well and nobody recognised her until a freelance photographer who had already taken pictures of the princess spotted her in a bar. Alida quickly got the princess out but not before a picture was taken on the pavement. The two had to escape on bicycles but the next day the picture was on the front page of every Dutch newspaper.

Far from landing them in trouble, the adventure enhanced the reputation of the princess and of the work of the centre. Major Bosshardt became a famous woman, called the 'Mother Teresa of Amsterdam', having a wax model in Madame Tussaud's and winning of 'The Amsterdammer of the Year' award.

One last project remained to be completed before Major Bosshardt was ready to retire. She was concerned that there was no place for older residents of central Amsterdam to live in retirement. A complex of apartments to be rented at modest prices was needed in the area. It would cost a great deal to build and planning permission would be hard to obtain.

The Mayor of Amsterdam held a weekly surgery to deal with problems of his constituents, so Alida made it her business to be first in the queue each week to ask about planning permission for her new project. Every week the Mayor had to report little progress. The application had to make its way through many committees and processes. Alida persisted; every week her enquiry was the same. Eventually the Mayor yielded. Calling his staff together he insisted that the approved plans were to be on his desk within the next week. He had to get rid of this troublesome woman!

The project for the Goodwillburgh was to cost 8.5 million guilders. By the time it was opened Alida had raised all the money and had a small surplus.

When the time came for Alida to retire (she was, by then, Lieut-Colonel Bosshardt) she could not leave the scene of her work. She remained a resident of the red light district, offering guidance and help to the centre, speaking about the work and keeping its supporters up to date with all the developments. In her late eighties she moved into an apartment in the *Goodwillburgh* she had created.

Admitted to The Salvation Army's Order of the Founder and invested by her Queen as an Officer in the Order of the House of Orange Nassau, Alida remains the determined, individual, simple follower of the Lord Jesus. All the honours and awards have not affected her lifestyle and belief. She still knows that you serve God best by loving him with all your heart and loving your neighbour as yourself. 'Serving God by serving people' remains her creed.

Envoy Matthew

THE SCHOLAR

THE SCHOLAR
The story of Envoy Matthew

THE gospel of Jesus Christ is good news for all. But very few Muslims convert to Christianity. For an Islamic scholar to become a Christian is most unusual. In Islamic countries The Salvation Army respects the majority faith. It works mainly with the non-minority communities although it always offers practical help to anyone in need. That is why the story of Syed Mazhar Hussain Rizvi – known as Envoy Matthew – is so remarkable. It was originally told by Mrs Lieut-Colonel Grace Bevan, who, with her husband, served in India and Pakistan.

'A SALAAM alayi kum.' This courteous Islamic greeting from an elderly Christian preacher sitting near the steps of his Jerusalem church was given each day to a passing Muslim on his way to teach in the old part of the city. Instead of the traditional reply: *'Wa layikum a salaam,'* a stream of spittle would land at the preacher's feet. That was how the teacher of Islam responded until, worn down by the old man's unfailing courtesy, he began to wonder why the Christian remained polite despite the repeated insult. That was one small step on the road which eventually led him to Christ.

The teacher, a Muslim missionary, was a professor of Islamic studies. He bore the proud name of an honourable family of that faith. Syed Mazhar Hussain Rizvi claimed to be a descendant of Mohammed through the prophet's daughter Fatimah. His forefathers had migrated from Iran. Some were part of the Muslim forces which conquered the Sind, now a province of Pakistan, in AD 712. Some settled there but others travelled on and made their homes in the Jullader district of East Punjab in the state of India.

Syed's birthplace was the village of Dokoha Saadat, which is about three miles from the family home of the former President of Pakistan, General Zia ul Haq. The boy's gentle father was a devout Muslim of the Shi'a sect. He was so well-versed in the Koran and other Islamic writings that he had his own faithful disciples. Little Syed often sat with them and the faith of his forefathers took root in his heart, there in the heat and dust of his Punjabi village.

Sometimes the family made a trip into the town of Jullunder. Their only means of transport was by slow, creaking bullock carts or vehicles pulled by camels whose bells would be ringing at every step. The country was then under the control of the British Raj, but not much evidence of that was seen in Dokoha Sadaat, where life went on in exactly the same way as it had for centuries.

Living happily with his six brothers and one sister, Syed played games in the dust of a Punjabi summer. He heard the familiar call of the brain-fever bird which intensifies its song in the scorching months. He knew the sleek grey bodies and red heads of the tall cranes that stood in the ripening fields of wheat and corn which were worked by the labourers in his father's fields. Syed would join the village boys as they shouted, splashed and danced in the wonderful, cooling rains of the first monsoon showers. He would lie on his *charpoy* (roped bed) and gaze at the stars and the crescent moon hanging low on hot, still nights – the same crescent moon and star which was a symbol of Islam.

The kind voice of Syed's father was stilled for ever when the little boy was just seven years old and his dear mother died five years later. Now without parents, Syed, the youngest member of the family, came under the care and protection of his eldest brother. This brother took him to Karachi where he was to live in the Soldiers' Bazaar, attending Karachi Grammar School on Frere Street.

He was a good, industrious student, but he was not at all happy with the teaching of Christian missionaries, being jealous for his own faith. Much to his annoyance, his closest friend in this school was persuaded to become a Christian and adopted the name of Andrew. But this Andrew, unlike the apostle of that name, was not able to bring Syed to Jesus, although eventually his influence may well have played a part in Syed's conversion.

After passing his senior Cambridge examinations and gaining a BSc degree from Bombay University, Syed was persuaded to sail to England where he obtained a further science degree at Birmingham University. He lodged in a house near the university. At this time he became increasingly interested in Islamic studies and those of comparative religions. His brother had plans for him to study for a PhD degree in Berlin, but Syed chose rather to spend some time travelling and preaching in Europe. Months later he returned to Karachi and with a group of Muslim friends went to Egypt. There he taught in the Jamia Azhar, the oldest centre of Islamic learning in Cairo.

Here, in Egypt, the teeming crowds, the life-giving Nile and the desert beyond where the age-old Sphinx looks down were all in striking contrast to the sophistication of Europe. But still he found that life in the West or in the Middle East could not ease his turmoil of mind or satisfy his restless spirit. Later journeys took him to Mecca, the birthplace of the prophet Mohammed. Mecca is the chief city of Arabia, deriving its wealth from the thousands of pilgrims who assemble there yearly to offer *Hadj,* for the possession of the temple of Ka'ba gives Mecca a special sanctity in Muslim eyes. From the desert area of Mecca, Syed followed the route of Mohammed and his companions northward. In 11 days the prophet and his company had journeyed until they arrived at Al Medina Al Munawara – the 'illuminated city'. Now Syed too came to Medina, believing that amid its fruitful valleys and lush date palm groves he would find perfect happiness.

For nearly 12 years he lived and taught in the area, living in a private house and travelling daily to his college. Sometimes he varied his routine with a trip to the port of Jeddah, a bustling and thriving community. Syed was to perform the *Hadj* many times during his stay in Arabia. He felt a sense of awe when he made such a pilgrimage. He saw the excitement and deep religious fervour of the thousands who gathered there. But he could not honestly say that the act did anything for him spiritually. Rather it left him feeling empty and unfulfilled. So he decided to go to Jerusalem.

About this time he wrote to Andrew, his old friend of Karachi days, telling him something of the struggle that was going on in his soul. 'Why do you not study the Christians' Bible?' replied Andrew. 'He is not a true Muslim who has no honour for the *Injil, Tauret* and *Zabur* (Gospels, Law and Psalms). If you read and study these, you will come to know the truth that you are seeking, just as I did myself.' The Law Syed could identify with, also the Psalms read well, but the Gospels were another matter! All his teaching, his proud heritage and the memory of his devout father combined to make it almost impossible for him to accept the teaching of the Gospels. The greatest difficulty lay in having to accept Jesus as Son of God and Saviour, so although he read and studied the Scriptures, he was still left in perplexity of mind and spirit.

He had been taught that Christians had altered the Scriptures to support their claims that Jesus was the Christ in fulfilment of ancient prophecies. This was always at the back of his mind as he studied. When he told this story Syed would become animated, often breaking into Arabic to illustrate a point, contrasting the Koran with the Bible to demonstrate their similarities and contradictions.

It was in Jerusalem, as we have seen, that Syed was challenged by the attitude of the old preacher. After almost a year he agreed to speak to the Christian. Through him he began to study Greek and Hebrew, and in reading the Gospels he was especially impressed by John 1:1-14. Here was something which did not contradict similar verses found in the Koran: 'In the beginning was the Word . . . and the Word was God'. Yes, he could agree with that, but when he read further that the Word became the Christ who condescended to live as a man, all the old doubts came creeping back.

Nevertheless Syed began to ask questions regarding baptism, wondering whether he would indeed find the truth and peace of heart that he was seeking within the Christian fold. At that time he was smoking heavily and this was but one of the reasons why a Christian minister, who no doubt sensed Syed was still uncertain in his mind, refused to baptise him.

While in Jerusalem he visited, not for the first time, the Mount of Olives and one day, in anguish of spirit, he prayed for a sign. 'Suddenly,' he claims, 'I felt that a gracious person was near me, one full of kindliness and pity. I knew in my heart that it was the Christ whom I could not accept.' But still Syed was not ready to receive the reality of Christ for himself.

From Jerusalem he set out to travel in Africa, visiting the busy port of Mombasa and then going further into Kenya to meet with Muslims and Christians wherever he went. Then he felt the call of his homeland and crossed the Indian Ocean by boat to Karachi once again.

What changes he found! After the end of British rule his part of the country was now Pakistan (Land of the Pure) and the population mainly Muslim. Its creator, Qaid-E-Azam Mohammed Jinnah, had been followed by successive rulers. The city of Karachi had grown beyond recognition. He found a rapid growth of *bustee* areas (squatters' colonies) and of industries large and small. Everyone looked busy, there was little idleness and few beggars on the streets for even in the *bustees* they looked for work.

Syed arrived in 1964, four years after Karachi had lost its position as capital of the new country. First Rawalpindi, then the newly founded Islamabad had become the capital. There was a grand reunion with his eldest brother who had settled in Karachi with his family. There was so much to talk about! Yet despite the warmth of family and friends there was still a vacuum in his life and during the months that followed Syed became so utterly depressed that he resolved to end his life. This urge came to him while standing on the sea wall at Manori, Karachi. How easy, he thought, just to let the warm waters of the Arabian Sea close over him, taking him beyond life's troubles and sorrows. 'Suddenly,' recalls Syed, 'I felt again that same warm presence. I felt an invisible force holding me back. Everything grew so bright around me and I knew it was indeed the Lord Jesus who held me back. I knew he had some purpose for my life.'

At that time The Salvation Army was working in Karachi among the many people who had become refugees when the states of India and Pakistan were created. In the city many people were as sheep without a shepherd but help came from missionary officers who knew the Urdu language well. They made an instant impact on the community. With untiring devotion they began to establish corps and societies, visiting the many *bustees* that had sprung up. They felt the problems of the people, sought to alleviate their poverty and to give them the dynamism of a happy, salvationist spirit.

The divisional commander was used to spending time and trouble in helping inquirers of various religious and ethnic groups, but even he was amazed to be met by the white-robed patriarch who appeared one day framed in the doorway of his office. It was Syed. 'I am Maghir Hussain,' Syed announced, then parried the major's courteous greeting with the words: 'Muslim I was born, and in effect am, but let me tell you my story. I have spent many years in the Middle East in study and contemplation. As a result I embraced the teachings and person of Christ. I am a Christian. It only remains for me to be baptised. How do I go about it?'

In response the divisional commander sent him with an introduction to the Rev Charles Coleman, a Baptist minister, and some days later Syed again stood framed in the doorway of the divisional office. He appeared illumined by an inner light as he said: 'Brother, my new name is Matthew. I am a baptised follower of Jesus Christ.'

'Will you serve him? How will you serve him?' challenged the major.

'God wants me to offer myself to you for service in The Salvation Army,' was the reply.

The divisional commander called on the captain of the City Station Corps, in the Railway Colony, to care for the new recruit. The soldiers were both surprised and delighted to welcome a convert from Islam. Soon, however, the young captain confessed that he could not compete with the power, eloquence and charisma of his latest recruit! So with the approval of the territorial commander, it was arranged that Matthew should serve in Mahmoodabad until enrolled as a soldier, when he would be commissioned as an envoy and put in charge of operations there.

Matthew gladly rose to the challenge, eagerly reading every Salvation Army biography and book on Army organisation that headquarters could supply. His grasp of the English language and his energy made him a first-class recruit and faithful soldier. With pride he was enrolled and made envoy in charge of Mahmoodabad Corps in the slums of Karachi.

He gathered a group of some 35 children and started to teach them with the same thoroughness as he had taught his Muslim pupils. They were taught in the compound of the small quarters where Matthew lived. There was no corps hall. One day the divisional commander brought along an official from the Christian Children's Fund, an American child sponsorship programme. The visitor was impressed and his organisation decided to sponsor Matthew's children. More and more children wanted to be taught by the envoy. Nearby huts were bought and teachers enlisted to help teach in the school which had increased its intake to 375 children. Matthew was the first principal.

Matthew still had close ties with the grandchildren of his eldest brother and he was pleased they all had responsible positions in the community. He held their respect in spite of his leaving the fold and he was invited to family gatherings, especially the weddings. Sometimes he was called to pray for their sick relatives.

'A labourer is worthy of his hire,' said the envoy and, although he was of an age when he could sit back and take his ease, still he was restless to do something for his Lord to 'restore . . . the years that the locust hath eaten'. He spent six years in Essanagri, another crowded area in Karachi. With his helper Sergeant Nathaniel he ministered to 42 Christian families. At first there were only four families but the old-world courtesy of Matthew could not fail to attract people, and children recognised how much he cared for their welfare. During the week, 65 children gathered together and were patiently taught to read and write. But what they loved best was Matthew's story-telling time when they heard stories from the Bible.

Besides the children, adults were taught to read and write. At first Matthew bought their books for them, but later they were encouraged to buy their own.

What of the children in Mahmoodabad? An informal educational project was commenced in 1978 in what was then named Azam Town. This coaching centre catered for 550 boys and girls, attending in two sessions. Ages ranged from kindergarten to 10th grade and there was a staff of 17 locally recruited teachers. In addition there were vocational training classes, a boys' hostel and a dispensary. The buildings and busy programme were fitting testimony to the faithfulness of one man and the officers who share his inspiration.

The tall, spare figure of Envoy Matthew, wearing his neat, grey uniform, still soldiered on through the streets of Karachi, greeted with respect by Muslim and Christian alike. Wearing his learning with humility, he was always proud to call himself a disciple of Jesus Christ. To the end of his long life he remained a faithful Salvationist. His funeral took place within the movement he had joined and many came to pay tribute to this remarkable soldier of Jesus Christ and The Salvation Army.

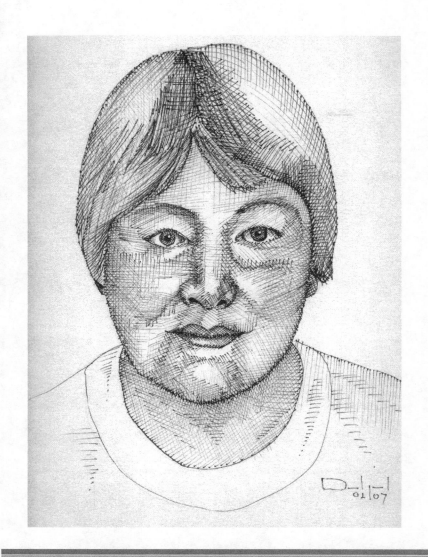

Nina Davidovich

THE HOSTAGE

THE HOSTAGE

The story of Nina Sergeevna Davidovich

EARLY in the morning of 22 June 2002 Nina Davidovich and three colleagues set out from Grozny in Chechnya. They had just opened a second leisure centre for the children of returning refugees. They left the children singing and dancing to the music at the centre and were sharing the happiness that it had brought to both children and parents. Suddenly the crack of machine-gun fire made their car lurch to a halt. They were surrounded by gunmen in camouflage, bundled into the back seats of their own car and that of the bandits and driven away.

Nina was most concerned for her friends. She felt responsible for them as she had led this team for two years. She saw the terror in their faces. They knew about the fate of hostages in Chechnya. Some time into the frantic journey which followed Nina managed to get into conversation with one of her captors. 'Please let my friends go,' she pleaded, 'You can take me if you must but they have done nothing to harm your cause.'

Perhaps the group had not bargained on four hostages, for Nina's prayers were about to be answered. After a frightening 20 minute drive the cars were stopped and Nina's friends were turned out of their car and left by the roadside. Only Nina remained captive but as she was hooded with a black bag and driven away she offered a prayer of thanks to God for the release of her friends. It was to be five and a half months before her ordeal was to end and she saw them again.

Nina was born in Leningrad in 1946, the daughter of a Red Army soldier who had seen active service in the Second World War.

93

Nina's mother and her three sons had survived the blockade of the city and then been evacuated to Siberia. Tragically the youngest son drowned in a river accident and Nina's mother grieved for him until the arrival of their beautiful daughter began to heal her hurt. Nina was a comfort to her parents, an intelligent, diligent child who gladly went to church with her Christian mother.

Churchgoing and the Christian faith were not encouraged in the Soviet Union. The bright student of mathematics and physics at the technical college was banned from going to church. Her father would have lost his job if the authorities had found out about his faith but Nina's mother continued to attend the church and prayed at home every day. She must have included her daughter in her prayers. Nina's childlike faith was soon lost in the atheist environment and she lived without the knowledge of a loving Heavenly Father. At the same time she was seeking for someone or something to trust. She dreamed of accomplishing great exploits but still looked for a teacher who could give direction to her life. The search for a real purpose in life had begun for her.

There were many disappointments on the way. Nina qualified as an engineer and a teacher but her relationships were in turmoil. A hasty marriage that proved unsustainable, broken relationships with her two sons and disappointments in her friends made for a very unhappy woman who was still waiting to see what she should do with her life.

In 1981 Nina experienced a real sense of God's love, tenderness and compassion for the first time. Although it was a long time before any obvious changes took place this longing for God proved to be something deep and lasting in her soul. She had begun to find a relationship with God. The One whom she had been avoiding for so long had broken through into her consciousness. She began attending different churches, first alone and then with a group of students from the technical college where she was teaching. In 1989 a second experience of God ended her doubts and in 1991, when she first attended a Salvation Army meeting, she found that the long search had ended. She had discovered her spiritual home.

At first the Army didn't seem like a church at all. There was none of the usual paraphernalia of church worship. Instead she found a group of people who wanted to express their faith by being helpful to others in need. There were plenty of people like that in Russia at the beginning of the 1990s. Nina soon became a Salvation Army soldier, learning from the Bible studies of Captains Geoff and Sandra Ryan, remembering the old stories from her childhood and seeing how clear and vital they were to her new found faith.

When the Army opened a service centre in St Petersburg Nina was invited to work as an outreach team leader and left her teaching post to concentrate on this new way of sharing the compassionate faith she had found. Her past experiences fitted her well for this task. As a teacher at the technical college she knew about the issues of drug taking among the students and the growing problem of HIV infection. Unlike other teachers she had found a way of discussing these matters with her students. In her new role for the Army she made friends with people working in rehabilitation centres and attended the open meetings of a Narcotics Anonymous group. Nina formed a group of volunteers from among the young Salvationists who visited schools, colleges and military academies to warn of the dangers of HIV infection. Her new work was so demanding that Nina became unaware of the continuing conflict in the Caucasus that was dominating the news in Russia.

Then at the beginning of 2000 Nina received a message from Captain Geoff Ryan, who was now working in Rostov-on-Don. Would Nina go to the small republic of Ingushetia for a couple of months to help set up a training programme for the children of Chechen refugees. Nina agreed and events moved very quickly. Soon she was living as a lodger with an Ingush family in Nazran, the village that is the capital of the republic. Before long she was accepted as a member of the family. Already a feeding programme for young children had been started. Nina spent time distributing the food in the villages and listening to the stories of people whose lives had been so damaged by the war.

She found that most of the children had had no schooling for several years, possessed no toys or books, had seen no films and shared no songs. Nina suggested that three small schools should be established in the camps, each catering for 50 to 60 children. She thought it would not be difficult to find suitable teachers and premises. The authorities provided large tents, improvised desks and chairs were made by the local men and soon over a thousand children's names were listed for the first school. Incredibly Nina and her team obtained textbooks and found teachers from among the refugees and over 1,500 children attended the schools.

It was not only basic education that was provided. After school hobby groups drew, knitted, made dolls, carved wood and made quilts. Lunches were provided and during the holidays the classes continued in the open air by the river. What started as a short trip for Nina turned into a long-term commitment, despite the problems of a climate that was difficult for her with its very hot summers and freezing winters.

The success of this venture was not without its problems. The Ryans had to return to Canada and the local Chechen co-ordinator of the Army's project was uncooperative. In the Muslim society of Chechnya the idea of a woman running such a large project was unacceptable. Nina had many threats against her but the never-ending demands of the work and her commitment to the young people whose lives had been so damaged kept her working far beyond any reasonable demands on her time.

Nina spent a great deal of time seeking to understand and to build relationships with the Muslim community. She read the Koran in a Russian translation and was given permission by the Mullah to introduce the Bible to her Muslim friends. What a surprise it was for them to discover that the story of Abraham,

96

whom they revered was also in the Christian Bible. Soon Nina and her friends were celebrating both Muslim and Christian festivals, praying together and discovering how much they had in common.

Nina's work became recognised by the United Nations and other international agencies. The Red Cross gave support knowing how efficient and unbiased was the distribution system in use. Then, after a year of rapid development, it became necessary for the programme to be taken over by a new organisation. Representatives from The Salvation Army World Service Organisation recommended that a local social organisation should be set up with Nina as its leader. Despite having little experience of establishing such an organisation Nina rose to the challenge and the Friendship Social Organisation was registered in Grozny, the capital of Chechnya.

The work grew and gained support from many international partners. Refugees now started returning to the rubble-strewn streets of Grozny. Nina and her team became concerned about the dangers faced by the young people. Armed gangs roamed the streets, unexploded shells were left in the ruined houses, there was little or no established security. Nina obtained permission to set up centres for the children of the refugees. Here they could be safe and their parents could leave them without anxiety.

It was when Nina and her colleagues had just set up the second such centre that she found herself ambushed by bandits on the outskirts of Grozny. She had read about people being kidnapped, seen films on the subject and read a UN booklet about how to behave in such a situation. She remembered that the advice was to remain calm and not to provoke any aggression. When her friends were released Nina found herself left with two guards who allowed her to remove the black bag from her head when the car stopped. Nina saw that her masked captors were young men. She decided it would be better not to know their identities so she invented her own names for them. As they waited for next instructions Nina invited them to play word games with her in a bizarre situation that seemed ludicrous to her at the time. Then another vehicle arrived, the guards were changed and Nina found herself with an older man. He told her that the kidnapping was no accident, her captors had been watching her for months and that a very large ransom would be demanded for her release. Nina did not want to think about what this would mean for her.

Once again Nina's calm attitude allowed her to make some kind of friendship with her captor. He told her about his family and his views on life. Carelessly the guard dozed off to sleep, leaving his machine-gun by his side. Nina is glad that she did not know how to use it for if she had killed him it might have provoked others to murder her.

That evening Nina was taken to a hideout in the forest and forced into a pit dug into the ground. Once again her face was covered by a plastic bag and her leg chained to a post. 'Your friends will have to pay a million dollars to get you out of here,' they said. It seemed so ridiculously large that Nina simply could not take it in. They left her with a thin mat and the darkness of the night. Nina said her prayers and tried to sleep.

The conditions in which she was forced to exist were terrible. Once the plastic bag over her head had been removed she could see, but there was nothing to look at. The light hardly penetrated through the gaps in the corrugated iron covering over her pit. Her only furnishings were a mat and a bucket. She was attacked by mosquitoes, mice and, to her great fear, sometimes by snakes. Her leg was chained to some heavy metal equipment giving her only the possibility of two short steps. She was often left for several days without food and without a visit from her captors. Worst of all was the endless nature of her captivity. When would it end? Would it ever end? Would she die in this hole in the ground or be shot by the people holding her? She knew that there was no possibility that the absurd ransom demand could be met. The loneliness of those never-ending days and nights would have broken the spirit of many captives.

If Nina was to survive she would need all the resources that God had given to her and, most of all, her unquenchable faith in the Lord who had saved and called her and whose work she had been doing.

From the very start Nina says that God gave her the wisdom not to think of the past, not to look for reasons why she had been captured, and not to blame herself for being careless and imprudent. She learned to live in the present and to try to keep herself together as a person. She established a regular routine. At 8 o'clock every morning she began with prayer and physical exercise. Then she had her meagre breakfast and began a pattern of meditation and reading. (The guards occasionally brought her old books and newspapers.) She hummed and sang to herself and tried to write poems. Some of these were poems for children and Nina was later to be able to give them to her granddaughter whose imminent birth was unknown to her at the time.

Then she wrote letters to her guards. She thanked them for the food and medications they brought her and for any words of encouragement that they occasionally offered. One of the guards whom she named 'Vado' responded to these letters and became sympathetic to her desperate needs.

Much of Nina's time was spent in prayer. She prayed for her family, especially for her sons, one of whom was still estranged from her. Little did she know that he was one of the people most actively searching for her. She prayed for her work, asking God to help her colleagues as they continued their work for the children of Chechnya. Of course, she prayed for herself. She asked God to be with her and not to leave her whatever was to happen to her. She asked for his divine protection and comfort. And she felt his presence with her. It was a marvel that she was kept from illness. She didn't even catch a cold when the autumn rains poured water into the pit or when the winter snows made her feel that she might freeze to death overnight.

Perhaps it was most remarkable that Nina found herself praying for her captors. She asked that he would give them mercy, to soften their hearts and to change their lives. They came to know that she was praying for them, they knew she was a Christian. Some even thanked her for her prayers.

The men who held her captive were involved in a cruel and vicious war. Nina learned that one who had been helpful to her and brought her food had been seriously wounded. Later another of them was killed and their colleagues asked Nina to share in the funeral meal – a Muslim custom. Nina became truly sorry for these young men. She remembered the words of Jesus:

'I tell you: Love your enemies, bless those that curse you, do good to those who hate you, and pray for those who despitefully use you and persecute you' (Matthew 5:44 *Authorised Version*). These young men had only known war, blood, brutality and dirt in their short lives. While it did not justify their crimes Nina was sorry that their lives had been lived in this way.

When the fasting month of Ramadan came to an end and her captors were celebrating the festival of Eid al-Futr, Nina wrote them a greeting card suggesting that they join in the old tradition of setting prisoners free on the day of a great religious holiday. Unfortunately it didn't work and with the approach of the winter months it was getting colder and colder in the tiny pit into which Nina had been moved. One of her captors brought her a quilt from home and another gave her an old sheepskin coat. He said she would never survive the winter without it.

Nina began to realise how tired she was. She had always known that there might be a tragic end to the story but she had hoped that her friends might find her and rescue her. Perhaps God would intervene on her behalf. She had learned from her guards that there had been a television programme about her plight and that many were searching for her. She could not have known that The Salvation Army had organised a world-wide network of prayer for her and that she was constantly remembered before God in thousands of homes and offices. Nor did she know that her friend, Captain Sandra Ryan had returned to the area to personally search for her.

100

Occasionally one of the guards would tell her, 'There is good news. You will be home in a couple of days.' This would give her a great lift of spirit and she would find herself smiling in her sleep. The disappointment when nothing happened was even more devastating. Once they told her that someone had offered a 200,000 dollar ransom for her and that there were talks with mediators about her release. None of this was true.

Just before the New Year the kidnappers became convinced that there would be no ransom paid. They told Nina that everything would decided in two week's time. Either she would be released or … ?

On the evening of January 6 2003 two of her captors came down to the pit.

'Get ready, you are going home,' they said. There was nothing to get ready but to unchain her leg, put another plastic bag over her head and drive her away in a car. When the car stopped she was taken out and led by the arm into snow-covered woods. Nina felt uneasy. Were they going to kill her? She prayed the Lord's Prayer over and over again. Then a car pulled up and she was bundled inside. Two more changes of car and then a man's voice said, 'Now you can take off the bag. Congratulations on your release.'

She was taken to a nearby town, allowed to wash off the dirt accumulated over half a year and shared in a festive meal. It was 7 January, the Christmas night for Orthodox Christians.

The next days were a round of press conferences, phone calls to family, friends and colleagues. How delighted they all were to discover that Nina was alive and well. Then followed a series of medical check-ups demanded by the authorities.

Nina insisted on going to Nazran where her colleagues were still working. There were tears in their eyes as they greeted her but Nina wanted to get straight back to work much to the concern of the UN people. They wanted her to go home to St Petersburg. They thought it was far too dangerous for her to stay in the Caucasus.

So Nina went home, but only for two weeks. She then returned to the Caucasus and to the work she loved. For the next year she continued to work in Grozny opening a new children's centre there and seeing the project established.

Since then Nina has had the opportunity to visit the USA to meet some of the people who had prayed for her. She has discovered all the activity that went on when during her captivity and was able to thank those who had prayed and worked so hard for her release. Then it was time to go home. It was hard to leave the team who had worked so hard and effectively for the children of Chechnya but new opportunities for service beckoned. She now heads the Salvation Army's Social Programme in Russia and still visits the Caucasus every year, finding great joy in the work that continues there.

What are the lasting effects of her captivity on this brave woman? She holds no grudges and bears no malice towards the Chechens. The love of God which sustained her through her ordeal has kept her from bitterness and anger. She wants to spend her days offering that love to everyone she meets.

Hilda Sigley

THE NURSE

THE NURSE
The story of Hilda Sigley

'MAJOR, please come at once. A baby has been born out in the mealie field and the mother needs your help.' It was not unusual for Major Hilda Sigley to be called to a birth. Sometimes the African women found that the baby was coming before they could complete the long, difficult journey to the clinic where she worked. But it was the middle of the night and the mealie field where this baby had been born was miles away from any road.

Hilda and an African nurse started out in their ancient truck. They got as near as possible to the place where mother and baby still lay in the field. Then it was a long, difficult walk over rough ground. There was no moon or starlight to guide them and the rocky ground was very slippery. Hilda cared for mother and baby in the darkness of the field, using all her skills as nurse and midwife. Then she began the long walk back to the truck. She cradled the baby in her right arm using her cardigan to provide warmth.

Balancing herself with her other arm, she clambered over the slippery stones. Once or twice she almost fell but at the critical moment she felt a strong hand firmly gripping her and helping her across. It was as though Jesus was holding her safely through a time of danger.

Hilda says it has often been like that for her. She has sometimes felt afraid – even out of her depth – but she has always found that God is faithful. He will not let you fall when you trust in him.

Hilda Sigley was born in a remote rural area of North Queensland, Australia in 1936. Her parents had a dairy farm and from her earliest days Hilda enjoyed working with the animals and just being around the farm. If she found an animal that was sick or injured she would take care of it and nurse it back to health. Life was very simple. There was no electricity and the family made its own pleasures. They were Methodists but the routine of the farm with its daily demand of milking the cows meant they were seldom able to get to church on Sunday. Hilda learned about Jesus from her mother but she did not really know him for herself.

School was a one-class place, sometimes with only seven children attending. Hilda did not like it much. Her teacher occasionally was cruel and she was discouraged from study until she learned how to work alone. She liked to be at home with her family and the animals. Most of all she loved being on her own in the solitude of this peaceful place. She was a quiet, even shy girl. The thought of being a hero never entered her head.

It was caring for the sick animals that prompted Hilda to think about becoming a nurse. Caring for people was something she would love to do. But nursing is more than just a useful job. It is a calling – a vocation. Hilda became convinced this was something she just had to do. Her mother was not too happy about her leaving home to train as a nurse. She had hoped she would marry a local farmer and settle down in the area. But Hilda set off for the nursing school and soon met a friend who became a great influence on her life.

Nancy Richardson was a Salvationist. She and Hilda joined the Nurses Christian Fellowship and soon Nancy invited Hilda to come with her to a meeting at the Salvation Army corps. The quiet country girl thought the meeting was noisy and boisterous. She did not like the idea of standing up and giving your testimony. Several times she vowed she would never go again but, somehow, she did. The young lieutenants at the corps encouraged her and soon the stories of Jesus that Hilda had learned from her mother became changed into a personal experience of his loving forgiveness.

Becoming a Salvationist was also a calling. Hilda felt sure this was something she had to do. Her parents were not pleased when she told them she was going to be a Salvation Army soldier. Their concern grew when she told them she had received a call from God and that she must serve him as a Salvation Army officer. How would this country girl cope in the crowded city? Could she really become an evangelist as well as a nurse?

The training college at Sydney might have been a million miles away from the family farm. Hilda had to adapt and do it quickly. She found some of the rules difficult to accept but the simple lifestyle at home meant college life was no hardship for her. The sessional name was 'Faithful' and Hilda found a text for herself in 1 Corinthians 10:13 – 'God is faithful. He will not let you be tempted beyond what you can bear.' She often remembered this when life was hard. It has always helped her to remain faithful.

Soon came her commissioning. Hilda found herself in the first of a number of appointments to maternity hospitals in Australia. Her midwifery skills developed and she learned how to be a member of a large staff of officers caring for the unmarried mothers who came to the hospital.

Hilda had often thought about using her nursing skills overseas but she had never done anything about it. Then, one day, she went to a meeting of the Salvation Army Nurses Fellowship. The speaker was Dr Frank Garlick, who had just returned from serving in India. 'The Army needs nurses in Africa,' he said. 'Don't ask why you should go, ask yourself why you should not do so.' Once again Hilda says the doctor's words were like a calling for her. She felt compelled to obey. She wrote to her leader offering her services if the Army wanted her. After a considerable time the reply came: 'Would you be willing to serve in South Africa?' Hilda said, 'Yes.' She felt that she must do so.

Hilda's first African appointment was to the William Eadie Hospital in Vendaland. This was many hundreds of miles away from the modern cities of South Africa. Vendaland was close to the borders of Zimbabwe and Mozambique. Its proud people, the BaVenda, had their own long traditions of lifestyle and culture. The William Eadie Hospital had been established for many years as a health centre caring for mothers and children. Hilda was to work with Major Nancy Bassett, a New Zealand officer-nurse who had worked at the centre for many years.

It was a considerable culture shock to live in this new community. Hilda was involved in a programme which often saw 200 babies born in a month. The story of her midnight visit to the mealie field was part of the 16-year appointment in this isolated place. Often the work of the hospital had to be maintained without a regular electricity supply. This was nothing new to Hilda. She had coped with this at home. But it made hygiene in the hospital very difficult and added to the other complications of life in rural Africa.

It was a good thing that Hilda and Nancy Bassett got on well together. They were both straightforward people who could adapt to the simple lifestyle that was needed. They could get on with their work even when they were short of resources.

Hilda learned to respect and understand the people among whom she lived. One day a laundry worker at the hospital saw Hilda using a sewing machine. The woman was amazed to see the neat stitches that repaired the torn cloth. She asked if she could learn how to work the machine. It took a long time and much patience but eventually the skill was learned and new opportunities as a seamstress were gained. Hilda also taught gardening and cooking to staff and patients, often producing wonderful meals from very limited ingredients and facilities.

Meetings and prayers at the hospital, the clinic and the nearby corps were part of the programme and Hilda took her turn in leading these occasions. She wanted the people to know about the Jesus she loved and served.

For 16 years Hilda worked at William Eadie Hospital. Then it was time for Nancy Bassett to retire. Local nurses were appointed to take over the leadership of the centre and to maintain the high standards and principles that Nancy and Hilda had established.

Hilda had every reason to return to Australia. Her parents were not in good health and needed her to help them adjust. She had fulfilled her calling. Surely that would be enough? But then she heard of a project that was urgently needed. From an informal settlement in the Kingdom of Swaziland a proposal had come for the Army to care for the very poor people who lived there. Hilda went to see the project. As she saw the desperate need of the people and the possibilities for the Army to commence work there she said to herself, 'This is it. This is where the Lord wants me to be.' The buildings were only just started and nothing was ready but the project caught her imagination and she volunteered to begin the medical work at the new centre at Mbabane.

The beginning of this new project was probably the hardest time of all her service for Hilda. Never had her sense of calling been put to such a hard test. She had always been used to a simple lifestyle and never minded going without basic necessities. But on her arrival at the new centre she found that neither the clinic nor her flat was ready. The African corps officers generously offered to find her a space in their tiny quarters. Hilda shared a bedroom with their four children and found privacy and solitude impossible to achieve.

Despite the kindness and generosity of her hosts Hilda felt close to tears. There was little opportunity to start the work at the unfinished clinic. She was effectively homeless. It was a dark time until another place was eventually found for her to stay. Gradually the new centre took shape and Hilda could begin her pioneering work.

The area was a shanty town with many people pouring in and building their own simple houses from whatever materials were available. Hilda visited the people in their homes and decided that the centre should offer a primary health care programme for the families. She set about recruiting and training the staff for the centre, treating them as equals and gaining their respect and love. The local Swazi nurses were wonderful in their commitment to the work of the centre. They were always prepared to go beyond their duties to care for the people.

Under Hilda's leadership – one *War Cry* article called her the 'Shanty Town Angel' – the reputation of the centre grew quickly. Hilda always insisted on the highest standards in everything the centre did. Soon people in the neighbouring areas were making the long journey to the Msunduza Community Centre because of the quality of care and treatment they knew they would receive.

As in her previous appointment Hilda used her farming background to good effect. She started her own vegetable plot and then taught her staff and patients how to add to their diet by growing their own food.

It was at this time that a new disease was beginning to be recognised in the area. HIV/Aids was taking a terrible toll of the young and previously healthy adults. As the numbers of victims increased Hilda recognised the need to take action. Following the example of work begun at Chikankata Hospital in Zambia she began a programme of visits and community-based care. There were no facilities for testing for HIV but it was important for the people to know about the risks involved. Hilda introduced a teaching programme using role-play and other methods. When she was able eventually to get access to a Government testing programme she was able to work with the results to help those who were coping with the dreadful disease. As the pandemic grew Hilda's centre was a place of hope in a desert of despair.

Life at the Msunduza Community Centre was always busy. In the middle of one of the hectic days Hilda was consulting patients at the clinic. Sad news arrived. Her mother had died after many years coping with dementia. Quietly and sympathetically one of the Swazi nurses took over the consultation and Hilda stepped outside for a couple of hours. She had never been afraid of being alone but at this moment she needed people around her. In the middle of her own grief she found peace of heart by going back to work to meet the needs of the many sick people she cared for. She was grateful that others had cared for her mother and she had work to do with those who relied on her care and skill.

A Salvation Army nurse in Africa needs to have many skills. Hilda designed new living accommodation for the senior nurses at the centre. One of those who came to live and work in the new accommodation was a young woman from Mozambique. She wanted to learn English so that she could enter training to be an officer. She spoke about her home country which was in the middle of a civil war. The stories of murder and rape and the suffering of the innocent people made a great impact on Hilda. The voice of Celeste was like the voice of God calling her to a new work.

Hilda discovered that the Army planned to open a new centre in a very poor area near to the Mozambique capital city of Maputo. They were looking for a leader for the work. To go to Mozambique was a great challenge for Hilda. It would mean a new language – Portuguese – and she knew something of the administrative problems of working in this country. She had always worked in poor neighbourhoods but never with the possibility of a violent conflict erupting around her. But God's call was clear. So, once again, Hilda volunteered for a new and difficult appointment. She would go to another shanty town near Maputo.

There were still outbreaks of fighting around the city but, in spite of the danger, many refugees were beginning to return to the area. Hilda set out on a programme to help them to settle and to return to farming their land. Sometimes, when they used the seeds and hoes they had been given, they would find the hastily buried bones of their friends who had been murdered by terrorists. Once again life was very tough for Hilda. The living conditions were primitive and she had to become used to everyone invading her privacy.

It had always been difficult for the Army to work in Mozambique. Official permissions were had to obtain. Hilda had

111

to start unofficially without the necessary approval. This did not stop her from reaching out to people in desperate need. Soon she was surrounded by many wanting her help.

Hilda began her work in Mozambique with her well-tried programme of visiting people in their homes. She taught crafts and skills to help people earn a little money. She formed Bible teaching groups especially for the women. She taught health, nutrition and hygiene and established a primary health clinic. Best of all she shared her love for Jesus. She found the poor people of Mozambique eager to become Christians. It was very moving to see so many coming to accept Jesus as their saviour. Many said it was the love and care they saw in Major Sigley that showed them a picture of the love of God for them in Jesus. Gradually the work of the centre developed and became established as a place of hope, joy and peace.

Twenty-eight years of service as a nurse to the people of Africa came to a sudden end when Hilda Sigley discovered she was suffering from cancer. It meant she had to return home and undergo treatment to save her life. It was a time of anxiety and frustration but the treatment was successful and Hilda was able to go back to her country home in Queensland.

Now she lives back in her own area. If you were to speak to the woman working in her garden or hosting the little Bible study group in her modest home, you would not realise that she had spent half a lifetime in another continent and that she numbered thousands of Africans as her friends. Many of these friends are alive today, prospering and healthy because of her care and teaching. Many have found the saviour she has served all her life.

One day she received a phone call from an Army leader in Sydney. Would she come to the congress to talk about her work? 'It might encourage the young people,' said the colonel. Hilda says it was a trick! When she arrived at the great congress meeting she found that the General was to admit her to the Order of the

Founder, the Army's highest award, for her courage, resolve and spirit of service.

She was surprised and overwhelmed by the reception she received. 'After all,' she said, 'I am no saint. I have often been out of my depth, sometimes afraid. But what could I do? I had been called! If I did not do it, who would?'

Joshua Ngugi

THE SHEPHERD

THE SHEPHERD
The story of Joshua Ngugi

THE young Kikuyu men were away from home looking after their goats. It was the first time these boys had been separated from their families. They were to look after the animals in the common grazing grounds belonging to the tribe. Each night they must bring them to the simple shelter and place of safety. The boys had built a hut in which to spend the night with branches from the trees. Now they were fast asleep, tired out from their hard day's work. A spark from the fire they had used for cooking set light to some of the huts and suddenly there was a huge blaze and many animals and huts were burned. The lives of the young men were in real danger.

Two of them, Joshua Ngugi and his cousin, woke up with a start to see the destruction around them. In the middle of the chaos they found that their hut and their animals had been spared. As they rushed to save their friends they realised it was little less than a miracle that they were safe. Joshua wondered why his life had been spared. Was it for a special reason that God had allowed him to survive?

Joshua was born in January 1916. He worked as a shepherd for his father's goats from the age of eight. The Kikuyu are the majority tribe of Kenya. Their main occupation was looking after the animals that were the wealth of the tribe. All the boys had to learn how to do this. They knew what it was to care for the goats that were sick and to make sure there was enough food for them to eat. The role of shepherd was an honoured role and Joshua thought that this would be his for the whole of his life.

117

When he was 14 Joshua was allowed to leave the family home and work in a wattle factory. It was a new and different experience for him. One day he was out in the fields when he heard the voices of a group of young women singing as they worked. The music was beautiful, almost heavenly, and he began to make out the words of the song: 'Yesu Nakupenda, Umali Yangu'. In the Kikuyu language the girls were singing, 'My Jesus, I love thee'. Entranced by the music, Joshua found himself weeping. The message had reached his heart.

The young women were students at a local Christian school working in the break between terms. He followed the group as they returned to their Scottish mission school. This was Joshua's first introduction to the Christian faith. He said, 'In all my lifetime I was not evangelised by a preacher. It was these singing girls and later The Salvation Army's *War Cry* magazine that led me to the Lord.' In his old age Joshua still weeps when he thinks about this special moment of revelation for him.

Meeting the Christians at the mission school made Joshua realise his need for education. His father disapproved of the idea. Along with his three older brothers his work was to be out in the fields caring for the animals. But one of his brothers recognised how valuable it would be for Joshua to go to school. He persuaded their father. Joshua would look after the animals each day before going to school and return to work after the lessons were ended. It would mean a long and demanding day's work but the benefits would be great. Joshua, the goatherd, had the opportunity to learn about caring for people.

Joshua proved to be a good student. He learned much from the Scottish mission laying a sound foundation of knowledge and understanding. He also shared in the worship of their God and began to understand this new faith. But it was really *The War Cry* that sealed his conversion. He came to realise he was a sinner and that he needed Jesus Christ as his Saviour. And so, one day, on his own, Joshua made a commitment to Jesus. He had become a

Christian. The singing of the girls in the field drew him, the mission school taught him, through *The War Cry* God spoke to him and now he knew the forgiveness and love of God for himself.

At that time becoming a Christian was a big step for a young Kikuyu man to take. Christianity was greatly feared and misunderstood in the village. Joshua found himself tested on many occasions. 'Declaring that you were a Christian was very dangerous,' he said. 'The villagers would beat you'. Even wearing Western style clothes could draw negative attention to you.

Then there was the question of coping with tribal customs. One day Joshua returned home to find that his father had killed one of the goats for a special meal with his friends. Joshua was expected to take part, including drinking alcohol and sharing in non-Christian rituals. He refused to take part and this made his father angry. It led to some family strife. Eventually Joshua would need to move on from his family home so that his faith could grow.

Joshua had to find money for his school fees and books so he found work first as a garden boy and then as a clerk to a white settler, keeping the books for his dairy farm. He began to think about his life's work and what Jesus would have him do. One day he took a walk during his lunchtime break. He says it was in the wilderness – perhaps it was an actual wild place or perhaps it was a wilderness in his soul. There he heard the call to be a preacher. 'I had a vision of myself preaching to many people and travelling to many places with the message of the gospel.'

Until this point the young man only used his Kikuyu name but as he studied his Bible he became especially interested in the Book of Joshua. He was so impressed by the life and work of the Old Testament leader that he took the name for himself. There was no christening or dedication ceremony. He simply wanted to serve God and to be used by him as Joshua was of old. So he became Joshua Ngugi.

The realisation of his vision of becoming a preacher had to wait for several years. Joshua had to prove himself in his work. He moved from one employer to another, and when his second employer died he continued to work for his widow. In addition to his official duties he developed a caring role for his employer, visiting her during a period in hospital, dressed in his Army uniform. The man who had been a shepherd for his father's goats was now caring for people. His employer was deeply grateful. 'Well done, good and faithful servant,' she said. Sadly this appreciation for Joshua's help became a dependence on the young African man that was to prove very difficult for Joshua.

Joshua had met The Salvation Army at Nakuru corps. Reading *The War Cry* he realised this was the church where God wanted him to serve and he became a Salvationist. It was here in a regular fellowship meeting that he met Bathisheba Muguri. They were married in 1937 and already knew they must respond to a call to full-time ministry as Salvation Army officers.

When Joshua told his employer of his intention to leave she was greatly disturbed. She did not want to lose this faithful servant and pursued him with a gun. Just like David, the shepherd king, Joshua had to hide from her anger. Later she took legal action to try to force Joshua to remain in her employment. Eventually the court agreed that Joshua and Bathisheba could leave. Joshua said, 'I did not return because my obligation was to the church.'

Finally Joshua and Bathisheba arrived at the training college in Nairobi and at the conclusion of their training were commissioned as officers in 1945. In those days life for Salvation Army officers in Africa was very demanding. They were expected to devote the whole of their time and energy to the work of spreading the gospel but there was no provision for a regular allowance for their needs. Indeed Joshua says it was not considered fitting that a minister should be paid for his work. So they simply trusted that the Lord would provide for them.

Working in poor communities meant they shared the hardship of the people. When food was scarce they had to find ways to improvise for their growing family. They devised many ways of disguising the lack of variety in their diet. Tea leaves were dried in the sun so they could be used again. Every part of an animal would be used in the cooking. Joshua and Bathisheba would often go without for the sake of their children.

While they were still young officers Captain and Mrs Ngugi were asked to undertake an appointment in Tanzania, far from their homeland. It proved to be a very difficult experience for them with some serious health problems for the family. However, they fulfilled the task they were given but it was with some relief that they were appointed back to Kenya.

Joshua was already fluent in his native language and in Swahili. He and Bathisheba were appointed to corps in many parts of the territory, speaking different local languages. Joshua made it his goal in every place to learn the new language so that he could share directly with his people. This would be a great blessing in later years when he had responsibility for the whole territory.

In the 1950s Kenya entered a time of great turmoil. There was great dissatisfaction with British colonial rule. Demands that the fertile land should be shared with the African people and greater representation of their needs in parliament led to an uprising especially among the Kikuyu tribe. Groups of Kikuyu protestors formed themselves into bands bound by secret oaths. They attacked white settler families and their loyal African servants. The Mau Mau rebellion meant that all Kikuyu were under suspicion.

It was a very difficult time for The Salvation Army. White missionaries were threatened and Government authorities reacted with cruel force against those they saw as their enemies. In this very violent and tense situation the Army needed African leaders who would show wisdom and courage in facing the ordeal. Joshua and Bathisheba Ngugi proved to be an excellent bridge between the many Kikuyu Salvationists and the white leaders of the territory. Their calmness and loyalty in the face of great provocation allowed the Army to stay united and focused on its main task of bringing people to Jesus. They were a wonderful example to their comrades. Joshua continued to minister to his own people, caring for their needs, understanding their grievances but speaking out against violence. The local authorities recognised the importance of their work and specially requested that they should be allowed to stay and work among their people.

On one occasion Joshua had been asked to go to a centre called Eldoret with three other officers. They were stopped at a checkpoint and, because they were all Kikuyu, were arrested by the police, who did not recognise the important work they were doing. In the heat of the moment they might have been beaten or even killed. Joshua's three colleagues were sent by truck to jail but the vehicle in which Joshua was being carried broke down on the way and before he arrived at the prison a senior officer from THQ negotiated the release of all four officers.

Throughout his ministry Joshua sought to speak to people about Christ. For those who did not know the Saviour he provided a welcome and an introduction to the Christian fellowship. His method of evangelism was simply to introduce people to Jesus, his saviour. In the same way that the simple song of the schoolgirls had attracted him, he tried by his life and his words to win others for Jesus. As a pastor he counselled those who were trying to live the Christian life. He believed that they must continue in their spiritual journey towards maturity. It was more important for Joshua to see his people grow in grace than for the Church to grow in numbers. To help in this process Joshua provided opportunities for fellowship in prayer meetings and Bible study classes. In this way the unity and health of the corps was maintained. He said, 'If you have many people but they are divided, then they will fall.'

From the earliest days of his officership it is clear that Joshua Ngugi was seen as a potential leader in The Salvation Army. He still treasures a letter written by Major Edward Osborne, one of the pioneer officers in East Africa, promoting him to the rank of lieutenant in 1946. The letter says, 'I know you will become a commissioner.' It would have been easy for Joshua to become over-confident of his abilities but through all the years of many appointments he retained his shepherd heart, caring more for his people than for himself.

In 1975 Joshua Ngugi was promoted to the rank of commissioner. Joshua became the first Kenyan to be appointed the territorial commander in his own territory. Then in 1977 he was the first African officer to serve as a member of The Salvation Army's High Council. His wide knowledge of his homeland and of the other countries which made up the East Africa Territory meant he was well placed to direct the development and growth of one of the most exciting parts of the worldwide Salvation Army.

The seven years of his leadership saw the territory grow in numbers until it became the largest unit in the world. This gave great joy to Joshua but his main concern was not the size of the territory but the spiritual growth of its officers and soldiers. Joshua was aware of the dangers of tribalism. He knew how divisive and damaging it could be if leaders favoured the members of their own group above others. Joshua was determined to stamp out any such practices within the Army. Such courageous leadership was often costly.

When he was aware of tribal problems, the territorial commander would follow up warning letters with personal interviews with offenders, first seeking as shepherd to show the way for the problem to be overcome. If this approach was rejected he did not shirk from disciplinary action. The unity of the Church was his first concern. It required constant and careful attention. There was no place for division and factions among its members.

The work of a territorial leader requires him to visit all the corps and centres within his charge. Commissioner and Mrs Ngugi were constantly travelling the roads of Kenya, coping with difficult journeys and often staying with officers in their quarters. When visiting, Joshua would emphasise family prayers, leading others in their devotions and establishing the regular practice in many homes. He loved to attend the open-air meetings at the corps he

123

was visiting. He believed in taking the gospel to the people where they were. He still feels this method of evangelism is important, despite the many changes in corps programmes that have developed over the years.

Commissioner Ngugi was not over-impressed by the phenomenal growth of The Salvation Army in Kenya in the years of his leadership and after. He did not take any credit for his emphasis on spiritual maturity and open-air campaigns that many consider to have led to the present success. His main concern was that people should know Jesus as Saviour and that growth in faith and unity in the congregations should continue.

Commissioner and Mrs Ngugi retired in 1982 after seven years leading their home territory. In retirement they went to live with two of their daughters and close to one of their sons a short distance from Nairobi where there is a small family farm. Joshua became an active soldier of Kikuyu Corps serving on the development committee which was seeking to raise funds for the growth of Kingdom through the corps. He continued to attend the corps meetings, regularly contributing the gift of his tithe from income or from the produce of his farm. This dignified man, always smartly dressed, made an impression on his neighbours. A woman remembered him visiting their home when she was a little girl. She recognised his spiritual authority even when he was making a pastoral visit to her father.

Joshua Ngugi was fluent in his native Kikuyu tongue and in the widely spoken Swahili and other local languages, as well as speaking some English. In his later years he would often revert to his native tribal language especially when speaking to his family. He loved to share his experiences with those who came to interview him and would need to be reminded to speak in the more easily understood Swahili language.

In 1998, at the age of 82, Joshua Ngugi was admitted to the Order of the Founder by General Paul Rader. The award marked the lifetime of service given by Joshua and Bathisheba and their contribution to the growth in grace as well as in numbers of The Salvation Army in Kenya. The certificate shared a place of honour in his home with a plaque bearing the following inscription: 'How beautiful and pleasant it is, when the members of one family live together in harmony. It is the crowning of the promised blessing of eternal life by the Lord.' More than any honour these words summarise the work of a true shepherd of his people.

127

THE CLOUD OF WITNESSES

THE stories in this book are of exceptional people who made great contributions to the work of The Salvation Army. They are heroes indeed.

But the Army does not consist of a few exceptional people. Its genius has been to harness the enthusiasm, commitment and loyalty of thousands of ordinary people. Their life's work has been to offer to God, through this movement, their loving service. The people whose brief stories are told in this closing chapter are representative of a far larger group whose names are recorded only in Heaven.

William Ough served as a corps officer in the British Territory without a break for over 43 years. He led 29 different corps, from some of the smallest to some of the largest. This meant that his family – he remarried after the death of his first wife – was uprooted on average every 18 months throughout his active officership.

In some of the larger corps where he was stationed he cared for over 300 soldiers, with many other people also on his visiting list. He would often preach at three meetings every Sunday and attend three open-air meetings. He loved to bring salvation and holiness messages to his congregations. His regular weekly ministry with *The War Cry* in public houses brought him into contact with thousands of people.

He never owned a car and did all his pastoral visitation by bicycle. Every one of the hundreds of soldiers in his corps received a regular visit. He was never afraid to challenge the complacency of some of the larger corps, encouraging young people to consider officership for themselves. He was a person of integrity and conviction. Someone who knew him described him as 'a revered gentleman, faithful servant and splendid warrior of the Cross'. He is typical of a generation of corps officers who loved God, loved the people he served, and loved the Army.

Amosi Mnyampi came from a small community in rural Tanzania. Although he received some Christian education it was not until he met pioneer Salvationists Frank and Jessie Dare that he began to take an interest in the faith.

He travelled many miles to attend the Army meetings as often as he could and one Sunday made his commitment to Christ as his Saviour. It was some time before his wife became a Christian but when she did they were the first couple in Tanzania to stand beneath the flag in an Army wedding ceremony.

A few months later Amosi disappeared from the corps and Frank Dare was concerned. Dare had no need to be worried. Amosi had returned to his own people and had commenced an Army outpost in his home town. From this beginning Amosi became one of pioneer officers in his homeland and eventually the leader of corps work in Tanzania. Today his son serves as a leading officer in Africa.

George Raddon came from a poor family who had to move from their native Cornwall to South Wales to find work. George left school at the age of 11 to become a carpenter and joiner. He was a very shy boy with a hasty temper that he had to learn to control. His mother had been introduced to the Home League at a small corps and George himself was soundly converted at the age of 11. He soon became involved in the work of the corps, learning to play an instrument and then teaching other lads.

While at an open-air meeting he noticed a pretty young woman with beautiful hair. Nancy was a member and the organist at the Apostolic church. She became George's wife and, eventually, a fellow soldier at Llanelli Citadel Corps. Their influence in the corps was immense. They were both strong and faithful local officers.

Everyone looked up to them. George served as the recruiting sergeant for many years and later as the band sergeant. He was a devoted Bible student, and a sensitive personal counsellor. Nancy became the home league secretary, ministering to many women who had no other Christian connections. Her practical concern led to the establishment of a luncheon club which she organised. Early each Sunday morning George would be found, with four or five others earnestly praying for the Lord's blessing on the busy day's activity.

Perhaps their greatest influence was on their family of six daughters. Their inheritance was a passion for godly living and their children and grandchildren remember the joy and enthusiasm for the gospel that they shared. No one could doubt that God was the master of their lives. They are typical of many thousands of soldiers and local officers whose commitment and integrity made the Army.

Mrs Rebecca Fuller was a faithful soldier and local officer in the Army's most remote outpost on the island of St Helena. This corps is nearly 2,000 miles by sea from its Territorial Headquarters in South Africa. Despite her isolation from other Salvationists Rebecca showed the very highest qualities of Christian service. She served as the corps secretary of Jamestown Corps until well into her 80s.

Her profession was the making of exquisite handmade lace. She used the same well-worn pins that had served her for many years. Her lace was sold on to many famous and wealthy people but Mrs Fuller continued to live a very simple life. She was always an active Salvationist and a meticulous local officer, but her most endearing qualities were her simple faith, shown by the way she lived, and her concern for other people.

She chose to live in a single room next to the Army hall, having sold her own house and donated the proceeds from the sale and from her work to helping needy people in South Africa. When a visiting officer brought her six apples she only kept one half of an

131

apple for herself and gave the rest away to neighbours. Every Sunday evening after the meeting she would carefully fold her uniform and place it in the same cardboard box that had brought it from London more than 40 years before.

Her faithful service was honoured by the Governor of St Helena and by The Salvation Army. She was admitted to the Order of the Founder in 1966. However, the true reward for her faithfulness is to be found in the approval of her Saviour.

Jane Smith had been an Army officer in her youth but returned to her home in Cumbria to look after her mother. After her marriage she went to live in Craigneuk, in Scotland. There she served as an envoy for 25 years, looking after some of the smallest corps.

When she retired from this task she became a legend as a Salvationist hospital visitor. With bundles of Christian literature and novels in her satchel she regularly visited many large hospitals in west central Scotland. Her pastoral care was always shown in practical ways. She established contacts with children separated from their mothers by illness, taking messages, gifts and love to all those affected. So well known did she become that she gained a nickname as 'Mrs God-bless-you'. Jane never had much money but was always willing to spend her pension on those she cared for.

Her service was recognised by the Army after 60 years of service but the most wonderful tribute to her was the crowd that lined the streets as her coffin was marched by the Army band to its final resting place.

Millie Chambers is a soldier at Kingston Central Corps in Jamaica. She is now an elderly woman and has to cope with considerable health problems. This does not deter her from her commitment to the Lord and to the people of her city. For many years Millie has helped on the regular soup run for the homeless people of Kingston. Accompanied by the officers from the social centre she spends two evenings a week visiting the places where homeless people gather. Millie knows her regulars well. She knows them by name. She has a supply of clothes that are to be given away and knows the genuine ones who will use the clothing and those who will simply sell it to get money from drink or drugs. When one of her 'regulars' is missing she will find out from others what has happened to the man and save food and clothes until he can be located. Her constant response to every enquiry about her health is that God is good. She rejoices in every day that the Lord gives to her.

Leontine Gorska was a senior Salvation Army officer in Latvia when the Red Army marched in to annexe the country in 1940. The Swedish divisional commander was expelled but a letter sent by Leontine and two other officers to the Russian authorities meant that the Army was allowed to continue its work. But in the summer of 1941 the Germans invaded Latvia and another period of occupation began. Soon the Gestapo ordered the immediate closure of all Salvation Army work.

Leontine had the presence of mind to rescue the deeds to the headquarters property and the drape from the rostrum of the Riga corps hall with its wording: 'Come to Jesus'. At great personal risk to herself she hid these precious things with her clothing. She could not have imagined that nearly 50 years would pass before she could return them to their proper place.

When the Germans left in 1944 the Russians returned and The Salvation Army was forbidden to work in Latvia. Leontine still regarded herself as a Salvation Army officer so she trained as a nurse and used these new skills to care for those in need. Secretly she arranged to meet the former Salvationists and friends to celebrate birthdays and other special occasions. Those times of worship, prayer and fellowship maintained the bonds of Christian love that sustained the faith of her comrades.

In the autumn of 1990 the first Salvation Army meetings since 1941 again took place in Latvia and the next year the country declared its independence. Leontine was able to hand over the deeds which permitted the Army to regain ownership of the one-time headquarters property. When the corps hall was renovated the rostrum drape was at last restored to its place of honour.

Leontine was promoted to Glory in May 1997. Three years later the President of Latvia opened a home for street children in Riga and dedicated the building in memory of Leontine Gorska. One of her leaders paid this tribute to her:

'She was a gracious lady who always had the best interest of other people at heart. She served them tirelessly and with great humility, focusing always on the needs of others. She was truly a servant of God'.

Angelita Rosario comes from the Dominican Republic. She spent some years in New York, USA. Whilst there she met the dynamic corps in that city and became an enthusiastic Salvation Army soldier. She saw what could be done for the people in the poor district in which she was staying and remembered many people in similar need in her own country.

Later she returned to the little town of Cotui in the Dominican Republic. Despite several attempts the Army had never established any work in that land. So Angelita decided to do something about it. At first in her living room and then in her garage, she began to hold meetings and to raise money to provide for the children in her area.

She sent a message back to New York: 'I have started the Army.' It was some time later that an officer from Jamaica was able to visit and found 70 people at a meeting in Angelita's home. From that beginning the Army now has six corps, six outposts, three basic schools and a day care centre. Envoy Rosario still serves the people of her home town. The children crowd round for Sunday school and for the outdoor meals served with love by Angelita and her friends. The group who worship with her have found a vibrant faith that is making its mark on the community.

David Barker served in Men's Social Work appointments for all his years of service. For most of the time he and his wife were in charge of some of the largest and most difficult hostels for homeless men in Britain. They were often working with very limited staff and poor buildings but they cared for thousands of men who came through the centres for which they were responsible. Many of them found a new start in life and a relationship with the Saviour who could help them rebuild their lives. David's gentle, gracious manner, even when dealing with abusive and violent men, demonstrated the faith which motivated him.

He was a sensitive man with a gift for poetry and a deep and loving relationship with the Lord. It must have been difficult for him to face the attitudes of some of those he was called on to serve but he did so simply and with great respect for men in the grip of alcohol-related problems. His final appointment as Chaplain to the Social Services Department allowed his influence to be shared widely throughout Britain.

Thomas Maqili was the son of an Induna – a counsellor to the king – of the Mhlongo clan of the Nkumane tribe in Gazaland, Mozambique. His father was betrayed and sentenced to death and the family was disgraced. Thomas went to work as a labourer in South Africa. There he met The Salvation Army. He hoped he would be taught to read and write but in his first meeting he was guided to seek Jesus as his Saviour. Although he had not met Christians before and found the worship strange, he prayed. 'As I prayed it was as if the dawn came to me,' he said. 'There was no bright light but a gradual awareness that the Sun of Righteousness was rising in my life. I got the light then, and it has never left me since.'

Tom soon became an enthusiastic evangelist. He longed to take the gospel he had found back to his own people in Mozambique. Political difficulties made it impossible for him to do this at first but he trained as an officer and served for 20 years in various appointments in South Africa. He worked among children and among the mine-workers of the Rand. He loved pioneering the development of new corps and centres.

135

Eventually in 1926 Tom Maqili was appointed to Gazaland and shortly afterwards to lead the Army's work in his home country of Mozambique. There were many Mozambiquans who had become Salvationists during their years working in South Africa but the Government refused to recognise or welcome the official recognition of the Army. Salvationists were imprisoned for conducting meetings but Thomas led courageously, often making long and difficult journeys to inspire and encourage the growing centres.

For 21 years Tom Maqili led The Salvation Army in Mozambique. There were many times of great trouble and persecution but the work grew despite the problems. Today there are thousands of Salvationists in his homeland. Tom's fiery evangelism and powerful preaching were the means by which many people found the Saviour.

Dorothy Purser is the daughter of long-serving officer parents. They spent their lives working in the Caribbean and in Africa. Dorothy learned what it meant to be poor and hard-working from her parents but also discovered from them the joy and fulfilment that comes from doing God's will.

Her parents sacrificed for her to study pharmacy and to qualify as a nurse. Then she entered the Army's training college in London during the Second World War. Dodging the bombs and studying the doctrines prepared her for a dangerous voyage back to Jamaica and the commencement of a life of service.

After some years she returned to London for further nursing and midwifery studies and then began many years in this specialised field. She was the first black officer to be appointed as director of nursing in a major Salvation Army hospital in the USA. She became the founder and director of an innovative programme for unmarried mothers.

Her final appointment as Chief Secretary of the Caribbean Territory was also a groundbreaking appointment as the first national woman to hold that office. In retirement Dorothy is still involved in a caring and learning ministry. She has learned never to be afraid when doing the will of God.

There had been an active presence of The Salvation Army in Cuba for over 50 years when the socialist revolution took place on New Year's Day 1959. Although the Salvationists rose to the challenge of coping with the feeding of thousands of people in the initial period of disturbance it was not long before the new government closed all the Army's children's homes and forbade contact with Salvationists outside the country. The territorial headquarters in Jamaica was unable to send support and to receive any news of the Army in Cuba.

Many people assumed that all work in Cuba had been forced to close and that officers and soldiers were no longer able to serve and worship. This period of silence continued for over 13 years.

Then in 1973 a meeting of the Caribbean Council of Churches was held in Kingston, Jamaica. Colonel John Needham, the newly appointed leader of the Army in the region, attended. Before the first meeting the delegates were gathered together for a group photograph. Colonel Needham noticed a man dressed in rather shabby Salvation Army uniform and a battered cap. 'Who are you?' he asked and was told: 'I am Major Ramirez and I represent The Salvation Army in Cuba.'

The colonel was astonished. 'We still have 10 corps working and the officers have remained faithful even though they receive no allowance and suffer along with their people.' Through a time of great opposition and persecution the Salvationists had remained faithful.

This was the beginning of the gradual opening up of contact between the Salvationists of Cuba and their colleagues in other islands and countries of the region. Now a part of the Latin America North Territory, the two divisions of Salvation Army work in Cuba continue to grow and to proclaim the gospel. The faithfulness of the officers and soldiers during the hardest days has reaped its reward.

The writer of the Letter to the Hebrews tells of the 'great cloud of witnesses' that surrounded the early Christians. They were the heroes of the faith whose stories he had retold: Old Testament saints who looked forward to the coming of the Saviour. Their faithful courage was to be an inspiration for those who were to follow. We, too, are surrounded by heroes. They don't recognise themselves by that title but their lives are an encouragement to all who seek to follow Jesus as soldiers of The Salvation Army.